THE UNIVERSAL CHRIST

THE UNIVERSAL

CHRIST

HOW A FORGOTTEN REALITY CAN CHANGE EVERYTHING WE SEE, HOPE FOR, AND BELIEVE

RICHARD ROHR

CONVERGENT
NEW YORK

Unless otherwise stated, Richard Rohr uses his own translation
and/or paraphrase of Scripture. Father Richard draws from a variety of
English translations including the Jerusalem Bible (JB), New American
Standard Bible (NASB), New English Translation (NET), J. B. Phillips New
Testament (Phillips), Revised Standard Version (RSV), and The Message.
CAC practice is to reference chapter and verse for scriptural sources,
but not to identify precise translations.

"Love After Love" from *The Poetry of Derek Walcott 1948–2013* by Derek
Walcott, selected by Glyn Maxwell. Copyright © 2014 by Derek Walcott.
Reprinted by permission of Farrar, Straus and Giroux.

Library of Congress Cataloging-in-Publication Data is available upon request.

ISBN 978–1-5247–6209–4
Ebook ISBN 978–1-5247–6210–0

PRINTED IN THE UNITED STATES OF AMERICA

Book design by Andrea Lau
Jacket design by Sarah Horgan
Jacket photograph: (sunset) Menset Photography/Getty Images; (star texture)
Ievgenii Volyk/iStock/Getty Images

1 3 5 7 9 10 8 6 4 2

First Edition

I dedicate this book to my beloved fifteen-year-old black Lab, Venus, whom I had to release to God while beginning to write this book. Without any apology, lightweight theology, or fear of heresy, I can appropriately say that Venus was also Christ for me.

The only really absolute mysteries in Christianity are the self-communication of God in the depths of existence—which we call grace, and in history—which we call Christ.

—Fr. Karl Rahner, Jesuit priest and theologian, 1904–1984

I do not worship matter. I worship the God of matter, who became matter for my sake and deigned to inhabit matter, who worked out my salvation through matter. I will not cease from honoring that matter which works my salvation.

—St. John Damascene, 675–753

No despair of ours can alter the reality of things, nor stain the joy of the cosmic dance, which is always there.

—Thomas Merton, 1915–1968

Contents

PART 2
THE GREAT COMMA

THE UNIVERSAL CHRIST

Before We Begin

In her autobiography, *A Rocking-Horse Catholic,* the twentieth-century English mystic* Caryll Houselander describes how an ordinary underground train journey in London transformed into a vision that changed her life. I share Houselander's description of this startling experience because it poignantly demonstrates what I will be calling the Christ Mystery, the indwelling of the Divine

---

* When I use the word "mystic" I am referring to experiential knowing instead of just textbook or dogmatic knowing. The difference tends to be that the mystic sees things in their wholeness, their connection, their universal and divine frame, instead of just their particularity. Mystics get the whole *gestalt* in one picture, as it were, and thus they often bypass our more sequential and separated way of seeing the moment. In this, they tend to be closer to poets and artists than to linear thinkers. Obviously, there is a place for both, but since the Enlightenment of the seventeenth and eighteenth centuries, there has been less and less appreciation of such seeing in wholes. The mystic was indeed considered an "eccentric" (off center), but maybe mystics are the most centered of all?

Presence in everyone and everything since the beginning of time as we know it:

> I was in an underground train, a crowded train in which all sorts of people jostled together, sitting and strap-hanging—workers of every description going home at the end of the day. Quite suddenly I saw with my mind, but as vividly as a wonderful picture, Christ in them all. But I saw more than that; not only was Christ in every one of them, living in them, dying in them, rejoicing in them, sorrowing in them—but because He was in them, and because they were here, the whole world was here too, here in this underground train; not only the world as it was at that moment, not only all the people in all the countries of the world, but all those people who had lived in the past, and all those yet to come.
>
> I came out into the street and walked for a long time in the crowds. It was the same here, on every side, in every passer-by, everywhere—Christ.
>
> I had long been haunted by the Russian conception of the humiliated Christ, the lame Christ limping through Russia, begging His bread; the Christ who, all through the ages, might return to the earth and come even to sinners to win their compassion by His need. Now, in the flash of a second, I knew that this dream is a fact; not a dream, not the fantasy or legend of a devout people, not the prerogative of the Russians, but Christ in man. . . .
>
> I saw too the reverence that everyone must have for a sinner; instead of condoning his sin, which is in reality his utmost sorrow, one must comfort Christ who is suffering in him. And this reverence must be paid even to those sinners whose souls seem to be dead, because it is Christ, who is the

life of the soul, who is dead in them; they are His tombs, and Christ in the tomb is potentially the risen Christ. . . .

Christ is everywhere; in Him every kind of life has a meaning and has an influence on every other kind of life. It is not the foolish sinner like myself, running about the world with reprobates and feeling magnanimous, who comes closest to them and brings them healing; it is the contemplative in her cell who has never set eyes on them, but in whom Christ fasts and prays for them—or it may be a charwoman in whom Christ makes Himself a servant again, or a king whose crown of gold hides a crown of thorns. Realization of our oneness in Christ is the only cure for human loneliness. For me, too, it is the only ultimate meaning of life, the only thing that gives meaning and purpose to every life.

After a few days the "vision" faded. People looked the same again, there was no longer the same shock of insight for me each time I was face to face with another human being. Christ was hidden again; indeed, through the years to come I would have to seek for Him, and usually I would find Him in others—and still more in myself—only through a deliberate and blind act of faith.

The question for me—and for us—is, Who is this "Christ" that Caryll Houselander saw permeating and radiating from all her fellow passengers? Christ for her was clearly not just Jesus of Nazareth but something much more immense, even cosmic, in significance. How that is so, and why it matters, is the subject of this book. Once encountered, I believe this vision has the power to radically alter what we believe, how we see others and relate to them, our sense of how big God might be, and our understanding of what the Creator is doing in our world.

Does that sound like too much to hope for? Look back at the words Houselander uses as she strains to capture the sheer scope of what changed for her after her vision:

Everywhere—Christ
Realization of oneness
Reverence
Every kind of life has meaning
Every life has an influence on every other kind of life

Who wouldn't want to experience such things? And if Houselander's vision seems to us today somehow exotic, it certainly wouldn't have to early Christians. The revelation of the Risen Christ as ubiquitous and eternal was clearly affirmed in the Scriptures (Colossians 1, Ephesians 1, John 1, Hebrews 1) and in the early church, when the euphoria of the Christian faith was still creative and expanding. In our time, however, this deep mode of seeing must be approached as something of a reclamation project. When the Western church separated from the East in the Great Schism of 1054, we gradually lost this profound understanding of how God has been liberating and loving all that is. Instead, we gradually limited the Divine Presence to the single body of Jesus, *when perhaps it is as ubiquitous as light itself—and uncircumscribable by human boundaries.*

We might say that the door of faith closed on the broadest and most beautiful understanding of what early Christians called the "Manifestation," the Epiphany, or most famously, the "Incarnation"—and also its final and full form, which we still call the "Resurrection." But the Eastern and Orthodox churches originally had a much broader understanding of both of these, an insight that we in the Western churches, both Catholic and Protestant, are now only beginning to recognize. This is surely what John meant when he wrote in his Gospel, "The word became flesh" itself (John 1:14), using a universal and generic term (sarx) instead of referring to a single human body.* In fact, the lone word "Jesus" is never mentioned in the Prologue! Did you ever notice that? "Jesus Christ" is finally mentioned, but not until the second to last verse.

We cannot overestimate the damage that was done to our Gospel message when the Eastern ("Greek") and Western ("Latin") churches split, beginning with their mutual excommunication of each other's patriarchs in 1054. We have not known the "one, holy, undivided" church for over a thousand years.

But you and I can reopen that ancient door of faith with a key, and that key is the proper understanding of a word that many of us use often, but often too glibly. That word is *Christ*.

What if Christ is a name for *the transcendent within* of every "thing" in the universe?

What if Christ is a name for the immense spaciousness of all true Love?

What if Christ refers to an infinite horizon that pulls us from within and pulls us forward too?

What if Christ is *another name for everything*—in its fullness?

I believe that is what the "Big Tradition" has been trying to say, maybe without even knowing it. But most of us were never exposed to the Full and Big Tradition, by which I mean the perennial tradition, the wisdom of the entire Body of Christ—and specifically for this book, the integration of the self-correcting themes that are

---

* John Dominic Crossan makes this point rather convincingly in *Resurrecting Easter* (San Fransciso: HarperOne, 2018), a study of how differently Eastern and Western art understood and depicted the Resurrection. We delayed the publication of this book so I could include his artistic, historic, and archaeological evidence for what I am trying to say theologically.

constantly recurring and reaffirming one another in Orthodoxy, Catholicism, and the many brands of Protestantism. I know that is a huge goal, but do we have any choice now? If we emphasize the real essentials of faith, and not the accidentals, it is actually not so hard to do.

If you will allow me in the pages to come, I want to be your guide in exploring these questions about Christ and the shape of reality for each of us. It's a quest that has fascinated and inspired me for over fifty years. In keeping with my Franciscan tradition, I want to ground a conversation of such immense scale in the stuff of earth so that we can follow it like a trail of crumbs through the forest: from nature; to a newborn child with his mother and father in a lowly stable; to a woman alone on a train; and finally, to the meaning and mystery in a name that might also be ours.

If my own experience is any indication, the message in this book can transform the way you see and the way you live in your everyday world. It can offer you the deep and universal meaning that Western civilization seems to lack and long for today. It has the potential to reground Christianity as a natural religion and not one simply based on a special revelation, available only to a few lucky enlightened people.

But to experience this new understanding, we must often proceed by indirection, by waiting, and by the practice of attentiveness. Especially as we begin, you must allow some of the words in this book *to remain partially mysterious, at least for a while.* I know this can be dissatisfying and unsettling to our egoic mind, which wants to be in control every step of the way. Yet this is precisely the contemplative way of reading and listening, and thus being drawn forward into a much Larger Field.

As G. K. Chesterton once wrote, *Your religion is not the church you belong to, but the cosmos you live inside of.* Once we know that the entire physical world around us, all of creation, is both the hiding place and the revelation place for God, this world becomes home, safe, enchanted, offering grace to any who look deeply. I call that kind of deep and calm seeing "contemplation."

The essential function of religion is to radically connect us with everything. (*Re-ligio* = to re-ligament or reconnect.) It is to help us see the world and ourselves in wholeness, and not just in parts. Truly enlightened people see oneness because they *look out from oneness,* instead of labeling everything as superior and inferior, in or out. If you think you are *privately* "saved" or enlightened, then you are neither saved nor enlightened, it seems to me!

A cosmic notion of the Christ competes with and excludes no one, but includes everyone and everything (Acts 10:15, 34) and allows Jesus Christ to finally be a God figure worthy of the entire universe. In this understanding of the Christian message, the Creator's love and presence are grounded in the created world, and the mental distinction between "natural" and "supernatural" sort of falls apart. As Albert Einstein is supposed to have said, "There are only two ways to live your life. One is as though nothing is a miracle. The other is as though everything is a miracle." In the pages ahead, I will opt for the latter!

Although my primary background is in philosophy and scriptural theology, I will draw on the disciplines of psychology, science, history, and anthropology to enrich the text. I don't want this to be a strictly "theological" book if I can help it, even though it has lots of explicit theology in it. Jesus did not come to earth so theologians alone could understand and make their good distinctions, but so that "they *all* may be one" (John 17:21). He came to unite and "to reconcile all things in himself, everything in heaven and everything on earth" (Colossians 1:19). Every woman or man on the street—or riding a train—should be able to see and enjoy this!

Throughout the book, you will find sentences or groups of sentences set off a bit from the paragraphs. Like these, related to our story above:

Christ is everywhere.

In Him every kind of life has a meaning and a solid connection.

I intend these pauses in the text as invitations for you to linger with an idea, to focus on it until it engages your body, your heart, your awareness of the physical world around you, and most especially your core connection with a larger field. Sit with each italicized sentence and, if need be, read it again until you feel its impact, until you can imagine its larger implications for the world and for history and for you. (In other words, until "the word becomes flesh" for you!) Don't jump too quickly to the next line.

In the monastic tradition, this practice of lingering and going to the depths of a text is called *"Lectio Divina."* It is a contemplative way of reading that goes deeper than the mental comprehension of words, or using words to give answers, or solve immediate problems or concerns. *Contemplation is waiting patiently for the gaps to be filled in, and it does not insist on quick closure or easy answers.* It never rushes to judgment, and in fact avoids making quick judgments because judgments have more to do with egoic, personal control than with a loving search for truth.

And that will be the practice for you and for me as we work our way together toward an understanding of a Christ who is much more than Jesus's last name.

PART 1

ANOTHER NAME

FOR EVERY THING

1

Christ Is Not Jesus's Last Name

*In the beginning God created the heavens and the
earth. Now the earth was formless and empty,
darkness was over the surface of the deep, and the
Spirit of God was hovering over the waters. And God
said, "Let there be light," and there was light.*

—Genesis 1:1–3

Across the thirty thousand or so varieties of Christianity, believers
love Jesus and (at least in theory) seem to have no trouble accepting his full humanity and his full divinity. Many express a personal
relationship with Jesus—perhaps a flash of inspiration of his intimate presence in their lives, perhaps a fear of his judgment or
wrath. Others trust in his compassion, and often see him as a justification for their worldviews and politics. But how might the notion of Christ change the whole equation? Is Christ simply Jesus's
last name? Or is it a revealing title that deserves our full attention?
How is Christ's function or role different from Jesus's? What does

Scripture mean when Peter says in his very first address to the crowds after Pentecost that "God has made this Jesus . . . both Lord and Christ" (Acts 2:36)? Weren't they always one and the same, starting at Jesus's birth?

To answer these questions, we must go back and ask, What was God up to in those first moments of creation? Was God totally invisible before the universe began? Or is there even such a thing as "before"? Why did God create at all? What was God's purpose in creating? Is the universe itself eternal? Or is the universe a creation in time as we know it—like Jesus himself?

Let's admit that we will probably never know the "how" or even the "when" of creation. But the question that religion tries to answer is mostly the "why." Is there any evidence for *why* God created the heavens and the earth? What was God up to? Was there any divine intention or goal? Or do we even need a creator "God" to explain the universe?

Most of the perennial traditions have offered explanations, and they usually go something like this: *Everything that exists in material form is the offspring of some Primal Source, which originally existed only as Spirit.* This Infinite Primal Source somehow poured itself into finite, visible forms, creating everything from rocks to water, plants, organisms, animals, and human beings—everything that we see with our eyes. This self-disclosure of whomever you call God into physical creation was the *first Incarnation* (the general term for any enfleshment of spirit), long before the personal, second Incarnation that Christians believe happened with Jesus. To put this idea in Franciscan language, *creation is the First Bible, and it existed for 13.7 billion years before the second Bible was written.**

When Christians hear the word "incarnation," most of us think

---

* Romans 1:20 says the same, in case you're wondering how this self-critique shows up in the Bible itself.

about the birth of Jesus, who personally demonstrated God's radical unity with humanity. But in this book, I want to suggest that the first incarnation was the moment described in Genesis 1, when God joined in unity with the physical universe and became the light inside of everything. (This, I believe, is why *light* is the subject of the first day of creation, and its speed is now recognized as the one universal constant.) The incarnation, then, is not only "God becoming Jesus." It is a much broader event, which is why John first describes God's presence in the general word "flesh" (John 1:14). John is speaking of the ubiquitous Christ that Caryll Houselander so vividly encountered, the Christ that the rest of us continue to encounter in other human beings, a mountain, a blade of grass, or a starling.

Everything visible, without exception, is the outpouring of God. What else could it really be? "Christ" is a word for the Primordial Template *("Logos")* through whom "all things came into being, and not one *thing* had its being except through him" (John 1:3). Seeing in this way has reframed, reenergized, and broadened my own religious belief, and I believe it could be Christianity's unique contribution among the world religions.*

If you can overlook how John uses a masculine pronoun to describe something that is clearly beyond gender, you can see that he is giving us a sacred cosmology in his Prologue (1:1–18), and not just a theology. Long before Jesus's personal incarnation, Christ was

---

* This is why the title for part one of this book says "Every Thing," instead of "Everything," because I believe the Christ Mystery specifically applies to thingness, materiality, physicality. I do not think of concepts and ideas as Christ. *They might well communicate the Christ Mystery, as I will try to do here,* but "Christ" for me refers to ideas that have specifically "become flesh" (John 1:14). You are surely free to disagree with me on that, but at least you know where I am coming from in my use of the word "Christ" in this book.

deeply embedded in all things—as all things! The first lines of the Bible say that "the Spirit of God was hovering over the waters," or the "formless void," and immediately the material universe became fully visible in its depths and meaning (Genesis 1:1ff.). Time, of course, has no meaning at this point. The Christ Mystery is the New Testament's attempt to name this visibility or *see-ability* that occurred on the first day.

Remember, *light is not so much what you directly see as that by which you see everything else.* This is why in John's Gospel, Jesus Christ makes the almost boastful statement "I am the Light of the world" (John 8:12). Jesus Christ is the amalgam of matter and spirit put together in one place, so we ourselves can put it together in all places, and enjoy things in their fullness. It can even enable us to *see as God sees,* if that is not expecting too much.

Scientists have discovered that what looks like darkness to the human eye is actually filled with tiny particles called "neutrinos," slivers of light that pass through the entire universe. Apparently there is no such thing as total darkness anywhere, even though the human eye thinks there is. John's Gospel was more accurate than we realized when it described Christ as "a light that darkness cannot overcome" (1:5). Knowing that the inner light of things cannot be eliminated or destroyed is deeply hopeful. And as if that is not enough, John's choice of an active verb (*"The true light . . . was coming into the world,"* 1:9) shows us that the Christ Mystery is not a one-time event, but an ongoing process throughout time—as constant as the light that fills the universe. And "God saw that light was good" (Genesis 1:3). Hold on to that!

But the symbolism deepens and tightens. Christians believe that this universal presence was later "born of a woman under the law" (Galatians 4:4) in a moment of chronological time. This is the great Christian leap of faith, which not everyone is willing to make.

We daringly believe that God's presence was poured into a single human being, so that humanity and divinity can be seen to be operating as one in him—and therefore in us! But instead of saying that God came *into* the world through Jesus, maybe it would be better to say that Jesus came *out of* an already Christ-soaked world. The second incarnation flowed out of the first, out of God's loving union with physical creation. If that still sounds strange to you, just trust me for a bit. I promise you it will only deepen and broaden your faith in both Jesus and the Christ. This is an important reframing of who God might be and what such a God is doing, and a God we might need if we want to find a better response to the questions that opened this chapter.

My point is this: When I know that the world around me is both the hiding place and the revelation of God, I can no longer make a significant distinction between the natural and the supernatural, between the holy and the profane. (A divine "voice" makes this exactly clear to a very resistant Peter in Acts 10.) Everything I see and know is indeed one *"uni-verse,"* revolving around one coherent center. This Divine Presence seeks connection and communion, not separation or division—*except for the sake of an even deeper future union.*

What a difference this makes in the way I walk through the world, in how I encounter every person I see in the course of my day! It is as though everything that seemed disappointing and "fallen," all the major pushbacks against the flow of history, can now be seen as one whole movement, still enchanted and made use of by God's love. All of it must somehow be usable and filled with potency, even the things that appear as betrayals or crucifixions. Why else and how else could we love this world? Nothing, and no one, needs to be excluded.

The kind of wholeness I'm describing is something that our

postmodern world no longer enjoys, and even vigorously denies. I always wonder why, after the triumph of rationalism in the Enlightenment, we would prefer such incoherence. I thought we had agreed that coherence, pattern, and some final meaning were good. But intellectuals in the last century have denied the existence and power of such great wholeness—and in Christianity, we have made the mistake of limiting the Creator's presence to just one human manifestation, Jesus. The implications of our very selective seeing have been massively destructive for history and humanity. Creation was deemed profane, a pretty accident, a mere backdrop for the real drama of God's concern—which is always and only us. (Or, even more troublesome, him!) It is impossible to make individuals feel sacred inside of a profane, empty, or accidental universe. This way of seeing makes us feel separate and competitive, striving to be superior instead of deeply connected, seeking ever-larger circles of union.

But God loves things by becoming them.

God loves things by uniting with them, not by excluding them.

Through the act of creation, God manifested the eternally outflowing Divine Presence into the physical and material world.* Ordinary matter is the hiding place for Spirit, and thus the very Body of God. Honestly, what else could it be, if we believe—as orthodox Jews, Christians, and Muslims do—that "one God created all things"? Since the very beginning of time, God's Spirit has been revealing its glory and goodness through the physical creation. So many of the Psalms already assert this, speaking of "rivers clapping their hands" and "mountains singing for joy." When Paul wrote, "There is only Christ. He is everything and he is in everything" (Co-

---

* See both Romans 8:19ff. and 1 Corinthians 11:17ff., where Paul makes his expansive notion of incarnation clear, and for me compelling. Most of us just never heard it that way.

lossians 3:11), was he a naïve pantheist, or did he really understand the full implication of the Gospel of Incarnation?

God seems to have chosen to manifest the invisible in what we call the "visible," so that all things visible are the revelation of God's endlessly diffusive spiritual energy. Once a person recognizes that, it is hard to ever be lonely in this world again.

A Universal and Personal God

Numerous Scriptures make it very clear that this Christ has existed "from the beginning" (John 1:1–18, Colossians 1:15–20, and Ephesians 1:3–14 being primary sources), so the Christ cannot be coterminous with Jesus. But by attaching the word "Christ" to Jesus as if it were his last name, instead of a means by which God's presence has enchanted all matter throughout all of history, Christians got pretty sloppy in their thinking. *Our faith became a competitive theology with various parochial theories of salvation, instead of a universal cosmology inside of which all can live with an inherent dignity.*

Right now, perhaps more than ever, we need a God as big as the still-expanding universe, or educated people will continue to think of God as a mere add-on to a world that is already awesome, beautiful, and worthy of praise in itself. If Jesus is not also presented as Christ, I predict more and more people will not so much actively rebel against Christianity as just gradually lose interest in it. Many research scientists, biologists, and social workers have honored the Christ Mystery without needing any specific Jesus language at all. The Divine has never seemed very worried about us getting his or her exact name right (see Exodus 3:14). As Jesus himself says, "Do not believe those who *say* 'Lord, Lord'" (Matthew 7:21, Luke 6:46, italics added). He says it is those who "do it right" that matter, not those who "say it right." Yet verbal orthodoxy has been Christianity's preoccupation, at times even allowing us to burn people at the stake for not "saying it right."

This is what happens when we focus solely on an exclusive Jesus, on having a "personal relationship" with him, and on what he can do to save you and me from some eternal, fiery torment. For the first two thousand years of Christianity, we framed our faith in terms of a problem and a threat. But if you believe Jesus's main purpose is to provide a means of personal, individual salvation, it is all too easy to think that he doesn't have anything to do with human history—with war or injustice, or destruction of nature, or anything that contradicts our egos' desires or our cultural biases. *We ended up spreading our national cultures under the rubric of Jesus, instead of a universally liberating message under the name of Christ.*

Without a sense of the inherent sacredness of the world—of every tiny bit of life and death—we struggle to see God in our own reality, let alone to respect reality, protect it, or love it. The consequences of this ignorance are all around us, seen in the way we have exploited and damaged our fellow human beings, the dear animals, the web of growing things, the land, the waters, and the very air. It took until the twenty-first century for a Pope to clearly say this, in Pope Francis's prophetic document *Laudato Si*. May it not be too late, and may the unnecessary gap between practical seeing (science) and holistic seeing (religion) be fully overcome. They still need each other.

What I am calling in this book an *incarnational worldview* is the profound recognition of the presence of the divine in literally "every thing" and "every one." It is the key to mental and spiritual health, as well as to a kind of basic contentment and happiness. An incarnational worldview is the only way we can reconcile our inner worlds with the outer one, unity with diversity, physical with spiritual, individual with corporate, and divine with human.

In the early second century, the church began to call itself "catholic," meaning *universal,* as it recognized its own universal character and message. Only later was "catholic" circumscribed by the word "Roman" as the church lost its sense of delivering an undivided and inclusive message. Then, after an entirely needed Reformation in 1517, we just kept dividing into ever-smaller and competing fractals. Paul had already warned the Corinthians about this, asking a question that should still stop us in our tracks: "Can Christ be parceled out?" (1 Corinthians 1:12). But we've done plenty of parceling in the years since those words were written.

Christianity has become clannish, to put it mildly. But it need not remain there. The full Christian leap of faith is trusting that Jesus *together with Christ gave us one human but fully accurate window into the Eternal Now that we call God* (John 8:58, Colossians 1:15, Hebrews 1:3, 2 Peter 3:8). This is a leap of faith that many believe they have made when they say "Jesus is God!" But strictly speaking, those words are not theologically correct.

Christ is God, and Jesus is the Christ's historical manifestation in time.

Jesus is a Third Someone, not just God and not just man, but God and human together.

Such is the unique and central message of Christianity, and it has massive theological, psychological, and political implications— and very good ones at that. But if we cannot put these two seeming opposites of God and human together in Jesus Christ, we usually cannot put these two together in ourselves, or in the rest of the physical universe. That has been our major impasse up to now. Jesus was supposed to be the code breaker, but without uniting him to Christ, we lost the core of what Christianity might have become.

A merely personal God becomes tribal and sentimental, and a merely universal God never leaves the realm of abstract theory and philosophical principles. But when we learn to put them together, Jesus and Christ give us a God who is both *personal* and *universal.*

The Christ Mystery anoints all physical matter with eternal purpose from the very beginning. (We should not be surprised that the word we translate from the Greek as *Christ* comes from the Hebrew word *mesach,* meaning "the anointed" one, or Messiah. He reveals that all is anointed!) Many are still praying and waiting for something that has already been given to us three times: first in creation; second in Jesus, "so that we could hear him, see him with our eyes, watch him, and touch him with our hands, the Word who is life" (1 John 1–2); and third, in the ongoing beloved community (what Christians call the Body of Christ), which is slowly evolving throughout all of human history (Romans 8:18ff.). We are still in the Flow.

Given our present evolution of consciousness, and especially the historical and technological access we now have to the "whole picture," I now wonder if a sincere person can even have a healthy and holy "personal" relationship with God *if* that God does not also connect them to the universal. A personal God cannot mean a smaller God, nor can God make you in any way smaller—or such would not be God.

Ironically, millions of the very devout who are waiting for the "Second Coming" have largely missed the first—and the third! I'll say it again: *God loves things by becoming them.* And as we've just seen, God did so in the creation of the universe and of Jesus, and continues to do so in the ongoing human Body of Christ (1 Corinthians 12:12ff.) and even in simple elements like bread and wine. Sadly, we have a whole section of Christianity that is looking for— even praying for—an exit from God's ongoing creation toward some kind of Armageddon or Rapture. Talk about missing the point! The most effective lies are often the really big ones.

The evolving, universe-spanning Christ Mystery, in which all of us take part, is the subject of this book. Jesus is a map for the time-bound and personal level of life, and Christ is the blueprint for all time and space and life itself. Both reveal the universal pattern of self-emptying and infilling (Christ) and death and resurrection (Jesus), which is the process we have called "holiness," "salvation," or just "growth," at different times in our history. For Christians, this universal pattern perfectly mimics the inner life of the Trinity in Christian theology,* which is our template for how reality unfolds, since all things are created "in the image and likeness" of God (Genesis 1:26–27).

For me, a true comprehension of the full Christ Mystery is the key to the foundational reform of the Christian religion, which alone will move us beyond any attempts to corral or capture God into our exclusive group. As the New Testament dramatically and clearly puts it, "Before the world was made, we have been chosen in Christ . . . claimed as God's own, and chosen from the very beginning" (Ephesians 1:3, 11) "so that he could bring everything together under the headship of Christ" (1:10). *If all of this is true, we have a theological basis for a very natural religion that includes everybody. The problem was solved from the beginning.* Take your Christian head off, shake it wildly, and put it back on!

Jesus, Christ, and the Beloved Community

The Franciscan philosopher and theologian John Duns Scotus (1266–1308), whom I studied for four years, tried to express this primal and cosmic notion when he wrote that *"God wills Christ first of all as the* summum opus dei, *or supreme greatest work."*† In other words, God's "first idea" and priority was to make the Godself both

---

* For a fuller treatment of this notion, see my earlier book *The Divine Dance* (New Kensington, PA: Whitaker House, 2016), which amounts to a prequel to this book.

† Scotism entry, *Encyclopedia of Theology,* ed. Karl Rahner (London: Burns and Oates, 1975), 1548.

visible and shareable. The word used in the Bible for this idea was *Logos,* which was taken from Greek philosophy, and which I would translate as the "Blueprint" or Primordial Pattern for reality. *The whole of creation*—not just Jesus—is the beloved community, the partner in the divine dance. Everything is the "child of God." No exceptions. When you think of it, what else could anything be? All creatures must in some way carry the divine DNA of their Creator.

Unfortunately, the notion of faith that emerged in the West was much more *a rational assent to the truth of certain mental beliefs, rather than a calm and hopeful trust that God is inherent in all things, and that this whole thing is going somewhere good.* Predictably, we soon separated intellectual belief (which tends to differentiate and limit) from love and hope (which unite and thus eternalize). As Paul says in his great hymn to love, "There are only three things that last, faith, hope and love" (1 Corinthians 13:13). All else passes.

Faith, hope, and love are the very nature of God, and thus the nature of all Being.

Such goodness cannot die. (Which is what we mean when we say "heaven.")

Each of these Three Great Virtues must always include the other two in order to be authentic: love is always hopeful and faithful, hope is always loving and faithful, and faith is always loving and hopeful. They are the very nature of God and thus of all Being. Such wholeness is personified in the cosmos as Christ, and in human history as Jesus. So God is not just love (1 John 4:16) but also absolute faithfulness and hope itself. And the energy of this faithfulness and hope flows out from the Creator toward all created beings producing all growth, healing, and every springtime.

No one religion will ever encompass the depth of such faith.

No ethnicity has a monopoly on such hope.

No nationality can control or limit this Flow of such universal love.

These are the ubiquitous gifts of the Christ Mystery, hidden inside of all that has ever lived, died, and will live again.

I hope the vision is coming clearer. It is in a way so simple and commonsense that it is hard to teach. It is mostly a matter of unlearning, and *learning to trust your Christian common sense,* if you will allow me to say that. Christ is a good and simple metaphor for absolute wholeness, complete incarnation, and the integrity of creation. Jesus is the archetypal human just like us (Hebrews 4:15), who showed us what the Full Human might look like if we could fully live into it (Ephesians 4:12–16). Frankly, *Jesus came to show us how to be human much more than how to be spiritual,* and the process still seems to be in its early stages.

Without Jesus, the sheer scale and significance of our deep humanity is just too much, and too good, for our ordinary minds to imagine. But when we rejoin Jesus with Christ, we can begin a Big Imagining and a Great Work.

2

Accepting That You Are Fully Accepted

I am making the whole of creation new. . . . It will
come true. . . . It is already done! I am the Alpha and
the Omega, both the Beginning and the End.

—Revelation 21:5–6

I tell you solemnly, before Abraham came to be, I AM.

—John 8:58

In these two scripture references, who do you think is speaking?
Is it Jesus of Nazareth, or someone else? We'd have to conclude
that whoever is talking here is offering a grand and optimistic arc
to all of history, and is not speaking simply as the humble Galilean
carpenter. "I am both the First and the Last," the voice says in Revelation 22:14, describing a coherent trajectory between the beginning and the end of all things. The second quotation, from John's
Gospel, is even more startling. If Jesus was the only one speaking
here—calling himself God while standing in Jerusalem's flagship

temple—the people present would've had every good reason to stone him!

While I don't believe Jesus ever doubted his real union with God, Jesus of Nazareth in his lifetime did not normally talk in the divine "I AM" statements, which are found seven times throughout John's Gospel. In the Gospels of Matthew, Mark, and Luke, Jesus almost always calls himself "the Son of the Human," or just "Everyman," using this expression a total of eighty-seven times.* But in John's Gospel, dated somewhere between A.D. 90 and 110, the voice of Christ steps forward to do almost all of the speaking. This helps make sense of some statements that seem out of character coming from Jesus's mouth, like "I am the way, the truth, and the life" (John 14:6) or "Before Abraham ever was, I am" (John 8:58). Jesus of Nazareth would not likely have talked that way, but if these are the words of the Eternal Christ, then "I am the way, the truth, and the life" is a very fair statement that should neither offend nor threaten anyone. After all, Jesus is *not* talking about joining or excluding any group; rather, he is describing *the "Way" by which all humans and all religions must allow matter and Spirit to operate as one.*

Once we see that the Eternal Christ is the one talking in these passages, Jesus's words about the nature of God—and those created in God's image—seem full of deep hope and a broad vision for all of creation. History is not aimless, not a mere product of random movement, or a race toward an apocalyptic end. This is good and universal truth, and does not depend on any group owning an exclusive "divine revelation." How different from the clannish form religion often takes—or the anemic notion of individual salvation for a very few on one minor planet in a still-expanding universe,

---

* See the extensive research on this term in Walter Wink's *The Human Being: Jesus and the Enigma of the Son of Man* (Minneapolis: Fortress Press, 2002).

with the plotline revolving around a single sin committed between the Tigris and Euphrates rivers!

The leap of faith that orthodox Christians made from the earliest period was the belief that this eternal Christ presence truly was speaking through the person of Jesus. Divinity and humanity must somehow be able to speak as one, for if the union of God and humankind is "true" in Jesus, there is hope that it might be true in all of us too. That is the big takeaway from having Jesus also speak as the Eternal Christ. He is indeed "the pioneer and perfector of our faith," as Hebrews puts it (12:2), modeling the human journey rather perfectly.

To summarize, because I know this is such a huge shift in perspective for most of us:

The full Christian story is saying that Jesus died, and Christ "arose"—yes, still as Jesus, but now also as *the Corporate Personality who includes and reveals all of creation in its full purpose and goal.* Or, as the "Father of Orthodoxy," St. Athanasius (296–373), wrote when the church had a more social, historical, and revolutionary sense of itself: *"God was consistent in working through one man to reveal himself everywhere, as well as through the other parts of His creation, so that nothing was left devoid of his Divinity and his self-knowledge . . . so that 'the whole universe was filled with the knowledge of the Lord as the waters fill the sea.'"* * This whole book could be considered nothing more than a footnote to these words of Athanasius!

The Eastern church has a sacred word for this process, which we in the West call *"incarnation"* or *"salvation."* They call it "divinization" *(theosis).* If that sounds provocative, know that they are only building on 2 Peter 1:4, where the author says, "He has given

---

* Athanasius, *De Incarnatione Verbi* 45.

us something very great and wonderful . . . you are *able to share the divine nature!*" This is Christianity's core good news and only transformative message.

Most Catholics and Protestants still think of the incarnation as a one-time and one-person event having to do only with the person of Jesus of Nazareth, instead of a cosmic event that has soaked all of history in the Divine Presence from the very beginning. This implies, therefore

- That God is not an old man on a throne. God is Relationship itself, a dynamism of Infinite Love between Divine Diversity, as the doctrine of the Trinity demonstrates. (Notice that Genesis 1:26–27 uses two plural pronouns to describe the Creator, "let *us* create in *our* image.")

- That God's infinite love has always included all that God created from the very beginning (Ephesians 1:3–14). The connection is inherent and absolute. The Torah calls it "covenant love," an unconditional agreement, both offered and consummated from God's side (even if and when we do not reciprocate).

- That the Divine "DNA" of the Creator is therefore held in all the creatures. What we call the "soul" of every creature could easily be seen as *the self knowledge of God* in that creature! It knows who it is and grows into that identity, just like every seed and egg. Thus salvation might best be called *"restoration,"* rather than the *retributive agenda* most of us were offered. This alone deserves to be called "divine justice."

- That as long as we keep God imprisoned in a retributive frame instead of a restorative frame, we really have no substantial good news; it is neither good nor new, but the same old tired story line of history. We pull God down to our level.

Faith at its essential core is *accepting that you are accepted!* We cannot deeply know ourselves without also knowing the One who made us, and we cannot fully accept ourselves without accepting God's radical acceptance of every part of us. And God's impossible acceptance of ourselves is easier to grasp if we first recognize it in the perfect unity of the human Jesus with the divine Christ. Start with Jesus, continue with yourself, and finally expand to everything else. As John says, "From this fullness (*pleroma*) we have all received, grace upon grace" (1:16), or *"grace responding to grace gracefully"* might be an even more accurate translation. To end in grace you must somehow start with grace, and then it is grace all the way through. Or as others have simply put it, "How you get there is where you arrive."

Seeing and Recognizing Are Not the Same

The core message of the incarnation of God in Jesus is that the Divine Presence is here, in us and in all of creation, and not only "over there" in some far-off realm. The early Christians came to call this seemingly new and available Presence "both Lord and Christ" (Acts 2:36), and Jesus became the big billboard that announced God's message in a personal way along the speedy highways of history. God needed something, or someone, to focus our attention. Jesus serves that role quite well.

Read 1 Corinthians 15:4–8, where Paul describes how Christ appeared a number of times to his apostles and followers after Jesus's death. The four Gospels do the same thing, describing how the

Risen Christ transcended doors, walls, spaces, ethnicities, religions, water, air, and times, eating food, and sometimes even bilocating, but always interacting with matter. While all of these accounts ascribe a kind of physical presence to Christ, it always seems to be a different kind of embodiment. Or, as Mark says right at the end of his Gospel, "he showed himself but under another form" (16:12). This is a new kind of presence, a new kind of embodiment, and a new kind of godliness.

This, I think, is why the people who witnessed these apparitions of Christ seemed to finally *recognize* him, but not usually immediately. *Seeing and recognizing are not the same thing.* And isn't this how it happens in our own lives? First we see a candle flame, then a moment later it "blazes" for us when we allow it to hold a personal meaning or message. We see a homeless man, and the moment we allow our heart space to open toward him, he becomes human, dear, or even Christ. Every resurrection story seems to strongly affirm an ambiguous—yet certain—presence in very ordinary settings, like walking on the road to Emmaus with a stranger, roasting fish on the beach, or what appeared like a gardener to the Magdalene.* These moments from Scripture set a stage of expectation and desire that God's presence can be seen in the ordinary and the material, and we do not have to wait for supernatural apparitions. We Catholics call this a *"sacramental"* theology, where the visible and tactile are the primary doorway to the invisible. This is why each of the formal Sacraments of the church insists on a material element like water, oil, bread, wine, the laying on of hands, or the absolute physicality of marriage itself.

By the time Paul wrote the letters to Colossae (1:15–20) and Ephesus (1:3–14), some twenty years after Jesus's era, he had al-

---

* Richard Rohr, *Immortal Diamond,* xxi–xxii, (San Francisco: Jossey-Bass, 2013), and the "mosaic" of metaphors in Appendix B.

ready connected Jesus's single body with the rest of the human species (1 Corinthians 12:12ff.), with the individual elements symbolized by bread and wine (1 Corinthians 11:17ff.), and with the entire Christ of cosmic history and nature itself (Romans 8:18ff.). This connection is later articulated in the Prologue to John's Gospel when the author says, "In the beginning was the Logos, and the Logos was with God, and the Logos was God. He was in the beginning with God. All things came into being through him, and *without him not one thing came into being.* What has come into being in him was life, and the life was the light of humanity" (John 1: 1–4), all grounded in the Logos becoming flesh (1:14). The early Eastern Fathers made much of this universal and corporate notion of salvation, both in art and in theology, but not so much in the West.

The sacramental principle is this: *Begin with a concrete moment of encounter, based in this physical world, and the soul universalizes from there, so that what is true here becomes true everywhere else too.* And so the spiritual journey proceeds with ever-greater circles of inclusion into the One Holy Mystery! But it always starts with what many wisely call the "scandal of the particular." It is there that we must surrender, even if the object itself seems more than a bit unworthy of our awe, trust, or surrender.*

Light and Enlightenment

Have you ever noticed that the expression "the light of the world" is used to describe the Christ (John 8:12), but that Jesus also applies the same phrase to us? (Matthew 5:14, "You are the light of the world.") Few preachers ever pointed that out to me.

---

* Richard Rohr, *Just This,* 7 (Center for Action and Contemplation, 2018), "Awe and Surrendering to It," 2018.

Apparently, light is less something you see directly, and more *something by which you see all other things.* In other words, we have faith *in* Christ so we can have the faith *of* Christ. That is the goal. Christ and Jesus seem quite happy to serve as conduits, rather than provable conclusions. (If the latter was the case, the Incarnation would have happened after the invention of the camera and the video recorder!) We need to look at Jesus until we can look out at the world with his kind of eyes. The world no longer trusts Christians who "love Jesus" but do not seem to love anything else.

In Jesus Christ, God's own broad, deep, and all-inclusive world-view is made available to us.

That might just be the whole point of the Gospels. You have to trust the messenger before you can trust the message, and that seems to be the Jesus Christ strategy. Too often, we have substituted the messenger for the message. As a result, we spent a great deal of time worshiping the messenger and trying to get other people to do the same. Too often this obsession became a pious substitute for actually *following* what he taught—and he did ask us several times to follow him, and never once to worship him.

If you pay attention to the text, you'll see that John offers a very evolutionary notion of the Christ message. Note the active verb that is used here: "The true light that enlightens every person *was coming* (*erxomenon*) into the world" (1:9). In other words, we're talking not about a one-time Big Bang in nature or a one-time incarnation in Jesus, but an ongoing, progressive movement continuing in the ever-unfolding creation. Incarnation did not just happen two thousand years ago. It has been working throughout the entire arc of time, and will continue. This is expressed in the common phrase the "Second Coming of Christ," which was unfortunately read as a threat ("Wait till your Dad gets home!"), whereas it should more accurately be spoken of as the "Forever Coming of Christ," which is anything but a threat. In fact, *it is the ongoing promise of eternal resurrection.*

Christ is the light that allows people to see things in their fullness. The precise and intended effect of such a light is to see Christ everywhere else. In fact, that is my only definition of a true Christian. *A mature Christian sees Christ in everything and everyone else.* That is a definition that will never fail you, always demand more of you, and give you no reasons to fight, exclude, or reject anyone.

Isn't that ironic? The point of the Christian life is not to distinguish oneself from the ungodly, but to stand in radical solidarity with everyone and everything else. This is the full, final, and intended effect of the Incarnation—symbolized by its finality in the cross, which is *God's great act of solidarity instead of judgment.* Without a doubt, Jesus perfectly exemplified this seeing, and thus passed it on to the rest of history. This is how we are to imitate Christ, the good Jewish man who saw and called forth the divine in Gentiles like the Syro-Phoenician woman and the Roman centurions who followed him; in Jewish tax collectors who collaborated with the Empire; in zealots who opposed it; in sinners of all stripes; in eunuchs, pagan astrologers, and all those "outside the law." Jesus had no trouble whatsoever with *otherness.* In fact, these "lost sheep" found out they were not lost to him at all, and tended to become his best followers.

Humans were fashioned to love people more than principles, and Jesus fully exemplified this pattern. But many seem to prefer loving principles—as if you really can do such a thing. Like Moses, we each need to know our God "face to face" (Exodus 33:11, Numbers 12:8). Note how Jesus said, "God is not a God of the dead but of the living *for to him all people are alive!*" (Luke 20:39). In my opinion, his aliveness made it so much easier for people to trust their own aliveness and thus relate to God, because *like knows like.* Some call it *morphic resonance.* C. S. Lewis, in giving one of his books the truly wonderful title *Till We Have Faces,* made this same evolutionary point.

The truly one, holy, catholic, and *undivided* church has not existed for a thousand years now, with many tragic results. We are ready to reclaim it again, but this time around we must concentrate on including—as Jesus clearly did—instead of excluding—which he never did. The only people that Jesus seemed to exclude were precisely those who refused to know they were ordinary sinners like everyone else. *The only thing he excluded was exclusion itself.* Do check me out on that, and you might see that I am correct.

Think about what all of this means for everything we sense and know about God. After the incarnation of Jesus, we could more easily imagine a give-and-take God, a relational God, a forgiving God. Strobe light revelations of Christ, which Bruno Barnhart calls the "Christ Quanta"* were already seen and honored in the deities of Native religions, the Atman of Hinduism, the teachings of Buddhism, and the Prophets of Judaism. Christians had a very good model and messenger in Jesus, but many outliers actually came to the "banquet" more easily, as Jesus often says in his parables of the resented and resisted banquet (Matthew 22:1–10, Luke 14:7–24), where "the wedding hall was filled with guests, both good and bad alike" (Matthew 22:10). What are we to do with such divine irresponsibility, such endless largesse, such unwillingness on God's part to build walls, circle wagons, or create unneeded boundaries?

We must be honest and humble about this: Many people of other faiths, like Sufi masters, Jewish prophets, many philosophers, and Hindu mystics, have lived in light of the Divine encounter better than many Christians. And why would a God worthy of the name God not care about *all* of the children? (Read Wisdom 11:23–12:2 for a humdinger of a Scripture in this regard.) Does God really have favorites among his children? What an unhappy family that would

---

* Bruno Barnhart, *Second Simplicity: The Inner Shape of Christianity* (Mahwah, New Jersey: Paulist Press, 1999), part 2, chap. 7.

create—and indeed, it *has* created. Our complete and happy inclusion of the Jewish scriptures inside of the Christian canon ought to have served as a structural and definitive statement about Christianity's movement toward radical inclusivity. How did we miss that? No other religion does that.

Remember what God said to Moses: "I AM Who I AM" (Exodus 3:14). *God is clearly not tied to a name,* nor does he seem to want us to tie the Divinity to any one name. This is why, in Judaism, God's statement to Moses became the unspeakable and unnameable God. Some would say that the name of God literally cannot be "spoken."* Now that was very wise, and more needed than we realized! This tradition alone should tell us to practice profound humility in regard to God, who gives us not a name, but only *pure presence*—no handle that could allow us to think we "know" who God is or have him or her as our private possession.

The Christ is always way too much for us, larger than any one era, culture, empire, or religion. Its radical inclusivity is a threat to any power structure and any form of arrogant thinking. Jesus by himself has usually been limited by the evolution of human consciousness in these first two thousand years, and held captive by culture, by nationalism, and by Christianity's own cultural captivity to a white, bourgeois, and Eurocentric worldview. Up to now, we have not been carrying history too well, because "there stood among us one we did not recognize," "one who came after me, because he existed before me" (John 1:26, 30). He came in mid-tone skin, from the underclass, a male body with a female soul, from an often hated religion, and living on the very cusp between East and West. No one owns him, and no one ever will.

---

* Richard Rohr, *The Naked Now* (New York: Crossroad, 2009), ch. 2. In fact, the holy name YHWH is most appropriately *breathed* rather than spoken, and we all breathe the same way.

Loving Jesus, Loving Christ

To be loved by Jesus enlarges our heart capacity. To be loved by the Christ enlarges our *mental* capacity. We need both a Jesus and a Christ, in my opinion, to get the full picture. A truly transformative God—for both the individual and history—needs to be experienced as both personal and universal. Nothing less will fully work.

If the overly personal (even sentimental) Jesus has shown itself to have severe limitations and problems, it is because this Jesus was not also universal. He became cozy and we lost the cosmic. History has clearly shown that worship of Jesus without worship of Christ invariably becomes a time- and culture-bound religion, often ethnic or even implicitly racist, which excludes much of humanity from God's embrace.

I fully believe, however, that *there has never been a single soul who was not possessed by the Christ, even in the ages when Jesus was not.* Why would you want your religion, or your God, to be any smaller than that?

For you who have felt angered or wounded or excluded by the message of Jesus or Christ as you have heard it, I hope you sense an opening here—an affirmation, a welcome that you may have despaired of ever hearing.

For you who have hoped to believe in God or a divinized world, but never been able to "believe" in the way belief is typically practiced—does this vision of Jesus the Christ help? *If it helps you to love and to hope, then it is the true religion of Christ. No circumscribed group can ever claim that title!*

For you who have loved Jesus—perhaps with great passion and protectiveness—do you recognize that any God worthy of the name *must* transcend creeds and denominations, time and place, nations and ethnicities, and all the vagaries of gender, extending to the limits of all we can see, suffer, and enjoy? *You are not your gender, your nationality, your ethnicity, your skin color, or your social class.* Why, oh why, do Christians allow these temporary costumes, or what Thomas Merton called the "false self," to pass for the substantial self, which is always "hidden with Christ in God" (Colossians 3:3)? It seems that we really do not know our own Gospel.

You are a child of God, and always will be, even when you don't believe it.

This is why and how Caryll Houselander could see Christ in the faces of total strangers. This is why I can see Christ in my dog, the sky, and all creatures, and it's why you, whoever you are, can experience God's unadulterated care for you in your garden or kitchen, your husband or wife, an ordinary beetle, a fish in the darkest sea that no human eye will ever observe, and even in those who *do not like* you, and those who *are not like* you.

This is the illuminating light that enlightens all things, making it possible for us to see things in their fullness. When Christ calls himself the "Light of the World" (John 8:12), he is not telling us to look just at him, but to look out at life with his all-merciful eyes. We see him so we can see *like him,* and with the same infinite compassion.

When your isolated "I" turns into a connected "we," you have moved from Jesus to Christ. We no longer have to carry the burden of being a perfect "I" because we are saved "in Christ," and *as* Christ. Or, as we say too quickly but correctly at the end of our official prayers: *"Through* Christ, Our Lord, Amen."

3

Revealed in Us—*as* Us

*To turn from everything to one face is to find oneself
face to face with everything.*

—Elizabeth Bowen, *The Heat of the Day*

If you've spent time in church, you've probably heard the story of Saul's conversion, as told in the book of Acts. It actually appears three times throughout the book (9:1–19, 22:5–16, 26:12–18), to make sure we don't miss how pivotal and newsworthy it must have been, and still is.

For years, Saul had savagely persecuted those who followed the way of Jesus. He was on his way to Damascus to do just that when, suddenly, he was struck down and blinded by what the text refers to as "light." Then, out of that light, he heard a voice saying, "Saul, Saul, why do you persecute *me?*"

Saul responded, "Who are you?"

And the reply came, "I am Jesus, and you are persecuting *me.*"

The deep and abiding significance of Saul's encounter is that he hears Jesus speak as if there's a moral equivalence between Jesus and the people Saul is persecuting. The voice twice calls *the people* "me"! From that day forward, this astounding reversal of perspective became the foundation for Paul's evolving worldview and his exciting discovery of "the Christ." This fundamental awakening moved Saul from his beloved, but ethnic-bound, religion of Judaism toward a universal vision of religion, so much so that he changed his Hebrew name to its Latin form, Paul. Later, he calls himself the "apostle" and "servant" to the very people he once disparaged as "pagans," "Gentiles," or "the nations" (Ephesians 3:1, Romans 11:13).

Paul, or perhaps a student under his training, says that he was "given knowledge of a mystery" (Ephesians 3:2) that revealed "how comprehensive God's wisdom really is according to a plan from all eternity" (3:10). He describes the experience as being like if scales had fallen from his eyes, so that "he could see again" (Acts 9:18).

In Paul's story we find the archetypal spiritual pattern, wherein people move *from what they thought they always knew to what they now fully recognize.* The pattern reveals itself earlier in the Torah when Jacob "wakes from his sleep" on the rock at Bethel and says, in effect, "I found it, but it was here all the time! This is the very gate of heaven" (Genesis 28:16).

For the rest of his life, Paul became obsessed with this "Christ." "Obsessed" is not too strong a word. In his letters, Paul rarely, if ever, quotes Jesus himself directly. Rather, he writes from a place of trustful communication with the Divine Presence who blinded him on the road. Paul's driving mission was *"to demonstrate that Jesus was the Christ"* (Acts 9:22b), which is why we are called "Christians" to this day, and not Jesuits!

Describing the encounter in his letter to the Galatians, Paul writes a most telling line. He does not say "God revealed his Son *to* me" as you might expect. Instead, he says, "God revealed his Son *in* me" (Galatians 1:16). This high degree of trust, introspection, self-knowledge, and self-confidence was quite unusual at that time. In fact, we will hardly see anything comparable till Augustine's *Confessions*, written around A.D. 400, where the author describes the inner life with a similar interest and precision. In my opinion, this is why the first fifteen hundred years of Christianity did not make much of Paul—he was so interior and psychological, and civilization was still so extroverted and literal. Except for the rare Augustine, and many of the Catholic mystics and hermits, it took more widespread literacy and the availability of the written word in the sixteenth century to move us toward a more interior and introspective Christianity, both for good and for ill.*

After his soul-blindness lifted, Paul recognized his true identity as a "chosen instrument" of the Christ, whose followers he used to persecute (Acts 9:15). In a move that could've seemed presumptuous, he presents himself as one of the twelve apostles, and even dares to take on *both* the Jewish leaders of his day and the leaders of the new Christian movement (Galatians 2:11–14, Acts 15:1–11) despite having no official role or legitimacy in either group. As far as I know, this self-ordination—not by lineage or appointment, but by divine validation—is unprecedented in these two sacred traditions, except for the few who were called "prophets" or "chosen ones." Either Paul was a total narcissist or he really was "chosen." This is the inherently unstable, even dangerous, role of true prophets. By definition, they do not represent the system, but draw their authority directly from the Source in order to critique the system. (Though

---

* Krister Stendahl, "The Apostle Paul and the Introspective Conscience of the West," *Harvard Theological Review* 56, no. 3 (1963), 199–215. This scholarly work is for me key to understanding how the last five hundred years largely misunderstood and individualized Paul's message. N. T. Wright will take the point even further in his marvelous and monumental study of Paul.

true prophets are somewhat rare, and Paul never applies that word to himself.)

But let's note Paul's primary criterion for authentic faith, which is quite extraordinary: *"Examine yourselves to make sure you are in the faith. Test yourselves. Do you acknowledge that Jesus Christ is really in you? If not, you have failed the test"* (2 Corinthians 13:5–6). So simple it's scary! Paul's radical incarnationalism sets a standard for all later Christian saints, mystics, and prophets. He knew that the Christ must first of all be acknowledged *within* before he can be recognized *without* as Lord and Master. (Forgive the male signifiers, but the sentence was too important to be complicated by qualifications!) God must reveal himself *in you* before God can fully reveal himself *to you*. Morphic resonance again.

It's important to remember that Paul, like us, never knew Jesus in the flesh. Like him, we only know the Christ through observing and honoring the depth of our own human experience. *When you can honor and receive your own moment of sadness or fullness as a gracious participation in the eternal sadness or fullness of God, you are beginning to recognize yourself as a participating member of this one universal Body. You are moving from I to We.*

Thus Paul shows the rest of us that we too can know Christ's infinitely available presence through our own *inner mental dialogue*, or the natural law, which is "engraved on our hearts." Quite daringly, he declares that even so-called pagans, "who do not possess the law . . . can be said to *be* the law" (see Romans 2:14–15). This is surely why he spoke to the well-educated Athenians of *"The Unknown God . . . whom you already worship without knowing it"* (Acts 17:23). Paul likely inherited this idea from the prophet Jeremiah, who dared to offer a "new covenant" (31:31) to God's people. But this idea remained largely undeveloped until a *natural law* was sought out by the moral theologians of the last century—and now in Pope Francis's strong understanding of individual conscience. It is still a shock to many.

But Paul merely took incarnationalism to its universal and logical conclusions. We see that in his bold exclamation "There is only Christ. He is everything and he is in everything" (Colossians 3:11). If I were to write that today, people would call me a pantheist (the universe is God), whereas I am really a pan*en*theist (God lies within all things, but also transcends them), exactly like both Jesus and Paul.

En Cristo

Paul summarizes his corporate understanding of salvation with his shorthand phrase *"en Cristo,"* using it more than any single phrase in all of his letters: a total of 164 times. *En Cristo* seems to be Paul's code word for *the gracious, participatory experience of salvation,* the path that he so urgently wanted to share with the world. Succinctly put, this identity means *humanity has never been separate from God*—unless and except by its own negative choice. All of us, without exception, are living inside of a cosmic identity, already in place, that is driving and guiding us forward. We are all *en Cristo,* willingly or unwillingly, happily or unhappily, consciously or unconsciously.

Paul seemed to understand that *the lone individual was far too small, insecure, and short-lived to bear either the "weight of glory" or the "burden of sin."* Only the whole could carry such a cosmic mystery of constant loss and renewal. Paul's knowledge of "in Christ" allowed him to give God's universal story a name, a focus, a love, and a certain victorious direction so that coming generations could trustingly jump on this cosmic and collective ride.

I hope that you will learn and enjoy the full meaning of that short, brilliant phrase, because it is crucial for the future of Christianity, which is still trapped in a highly individualistic notion of salvation that ends up not looking much like salvation at all. All of us, without exception, are living inside of a common identity, already in place, that is driving and guiding us forward. Paul calls this bigger Divine identity the "mystery of his purpose, the hidden plan he so kindly made *en Cristo* from the very beginning" (Ephesians 1:9). Today, we might call it the "collective unconscious."

Every single creature—the teen mother nursing her child, every one of the twenty thousand species of butterflies, an immigrant living in fear, a blade of grass, you reading this book—all are "in Christ" and "chosen from the beginning" (Ephesians 1:3, 9). What else could they be? *Salvation for Paul is an ontological and cosmological message (which is solid) before it ever becomes a moral or psychological one (which is always unstable).* Pause and give that some serious thought, if you can.

Did you ever notice that in the Gospel of Mark, Jesus tells the disciples to proclaim the Good News to "all creation" or "every creature," and not just to humans (16:15)? Paul affirms that he has done this very thing when he says, "Never let yourself drift away from the hope promised by the Good News, which *has been preached to every creature under heaven,* and of which I Paul have become the servant" (Colossians 1:23). Did he really talk to and convince "every creature under heaven" in his short lifetime? Surely not, but he did know that he had announced to the world the deepest philosophical ground of things by saying that it all was *in Christ*—and he daringly believed that this truth would eventually stick and succeed.

I have never been separate from God, nor can I be, except in my mind. I would love for you to bring this realization to loving consciousness! In fact, why not stop reading now, and just breathe and let it sink in. It is crucial that you know this experientially and at a cellular level—which is, in fact, a real way of knowing just as much as rational knowing. Its primary characteristic is that it is a non-dual and thus an open-ended way of knowing, which does not close down so quickly and so definitively as dualistic thought does.*

Regrettably, Christians have not protected this radical awareness of oneness with the divine. Paul's brilliant understanding of a Corporate Christ, and thus our cosmic identity, was soon lost as early Christians focused more and more on Jesus *alone* and even *apart from* the Eternal Flow of the Trinity, which is finally theologically unworkable.† Christ forever keeps Jesus firmly inside the Trinity, not a mere later add-on or a somewhat arbitrary incarnation. Trinitarianism keeps God as *Relationship Itself* from the very beginning, and not a mere monarch.

To legitimate our new religion in the Roman Empire, Christians felt that we had to prove that Jesus was independently divine. After the Council of Nicaea (325), Jesus was independently said to be "consubstantial" with God, and after the Council of Chalcedon (451), the church agreed on a philosophical definition of Jesus's humanity and divinity as being united as one in him. All true, but such oneness largely remained distant academic theory because we did not draw out the practical and wonderful implications. As a rule, we were more interested in the superiority of our own tribe, group, or nation than we were in the wholeness of creation. Our view of reality was largely imperial, patriarchal, and dualistic. Things were seen as either for us or against us, and we were either winners or losers, totally good or totally bad—such a small self and its personal salvation always remained our overwhelming preoccupation up to now. This is surely how our religion became so focused on obedience and conformity, instead of on love in any practical or expanding sense.

---

* Rohr, *The Naked Now,* and *Just This* (cac.org, 2017), a book of brief spiritual prompts and practices. Both develop this key idea.

† Rohr, *The Divine Dance.*

Without a Shared and Big Story, we all retreat into private individualism for a bit of sanity and safety.

Perhaps the primary example of our lack of attention to the Christ Mystery can be seen in the way we continue to pollute and ravage planet earth, the very thing we all stand on and live from. Science now appears to love and respect physicality more than most religion does! No wonder that *science and business have taken over as the major explainers of meaning* for the vast majority of people today (even many who still go to church). We Christians did not take this world seriously, I am afraid, because our notion of God or salvation didn't include or honor the physical universe. And now, I am afraid, the world does not take us seriously.

Hope cannot be had by the individual if everything is corporately hopeless.

It is hard to heal individuals when the whole thing is seen as unhealable.

We are still trying to paddle our way out of this whirlpool, and with a very small paddle! Only with a notion of the Preexisting Christ can we recover where this Jesus was "coming from" *and where he is leading us*—which is precisely into the "bosom of the Trinity" (John 1:18). "I shall return to take you with me, so that where I am you also may be" (John 14:3), the Christ has promised. That might just be the best and most succinct description of salvation there is in the whole New Testament.

A Paradigm Shift

In scientific and cultural thinking, the term "paradigm shift" describes a major switch in one's assumptions or viewpoint. We hear the term much less often in the world of religion, where groups assume they are dealing with eternal and unchangeable absolutes.

But ironically, a religious paradigm shift was exactly what Jesus and Paul were initiating in their day—so much so that their way of seeing became a whole new religion, whether that is what they intended or not. We now call this two-thousand-year-old paradigm shift from Judaism "Christianity."

History is still waiting for the Christian mind to "shift" back to what has always been true since the initial creation, which is the only thing that will ever make it a universal (or truly *catholic*) religion. The Universal Christ was just too big an idea, too monumental a shift for most of the first two thousand years. Humans prefer to see things in anecdotal and historical parts, even when such a view leads to incoherence, alienation, or hopelessness.

Every religion, each in its own way, is looking for the gateway, the conduit, the Sacrament, the Avatar, the finger that points to the moon. We need someone to model and exemplify the journey from physical incarnation, through a rather ordinary human existence, through trials and death, and into a Universal Presence unlimited by space and time (which we call *"resurrection"*). Most of us know about Jesus walking this journey, but far fewer know that Christ is the collective and eternal manifestation of the same—and that "the Christ" image includes all of us and every thing. Paul was overwhelmed by this recognition, and it became the core of his entire message. My hope is that this paradigm shift will become just as obvious to you.

Jesus can hold together one group or religion. Christ can hold together everything.

In fact, Christ already does this; it is we who resist such wholeness, as if we enjoy our arguments and our divisions into parts. Yet throughout the Scriptures, we were given statements like these:

- "When everything is reconciled in him . . . God will be all in all." (1 Corinthians 15:28)

- "There is only Christ. He is everything and he is in everything." (Colossians 3:11)

- "All fullness is found in him, through him all things are reconciled, everything in heaven and everything on earth." (Colossians 1:19–20)

This is not heresy, universalism, or a cheap version of Unitarianism. This is the Cosmic Christ, who always was, who became incarnate in time, and who is still being revealed. *We would have helped history and individuals so much more if we had spent our time revealing how Christ is everywhere instead of proving that Jesus was God.*

But big ideas take time to settle in.

A Fully Participatory Universe

I cannot help but think that future generations will label the first two thousand years of Christianity "early Christianity." They will, I believe, draw out more and more of the massive implications of this understanding of a Cosmic Christ. They will have long discarded the notion of Christian salvation as a private evacuation plan that gets a select few humans into the next world. The current world has been largely taken for granted or ignored, unless it could be exploited for our individual benefit. Why would people with such a belief ever feel at home in heaven? They didn't even practice for it! Nor did they learn how to feel at home on earth.

(*In calling out the limitations of this kind of gospel, I'm speaking primarily to privileged, mostly white Christians in the Northern Hemisphere. I don't for a minute forget how hard most people's lives have been in almost all of history. Life has been, and remains, "a vale of tears" for countless millions, and I can surely understand why only*

*the hope of a better world gave these brothers and sisters reason to put
one foot in front of the other and live another day.)*

No doubt you're aware that many traditional Christians today
consider the concept of universal anything—including salvation—
heresy. Many do not even like the United Nations. And many
Catholics and Orthodox Christians use the lines of ethnicity to
determine who's in and who's out. I find these convictions quite
strange for a religion that believes that "one God created all things."
Surely God is at least as big and mysterious as what we now know
the shape of the universe to be—a universe that is expanding at
ever faster speeds, just like the evolution of consciousness that has
been proceeding for centuries. How can anyone read the whole or
even a small part of John 17 and think either Christ or Jesus is about
anything other than unity and union? "Father, may they all be one,"
Christ says in verse 21, repeating this same desire and intention in
many ways in the full prayer. *I suspect God gets what God prays for!*

Along with *en Cristo,* Paul loves to use words like "wisdom,"
"secret," "hidden plan," and "mystery." He uses them so many times,
we probably jump over them quickly, assuming we know what he
means. Most of us assume he's talking about Jesus, which is partly
right. But the direct meaning of Paul's *secret mystery* is the Christ
we are talking about in this book. For Paul, Christ is "that mystery
which for endless ages has been kept secret" (Romans 16:25–27).
And a well-kept secret it still remains for most Christians.

As St. Augustine would courageously put it in his *Retractions*:
"For what is now called the Christian religion existed even among
the ancients and was not lacking from the beginning of the human
race."* Think about that: Were Neanderthals and Cro-Magnons,
Mayans and Babylonians, African and Asian civilizations, and the

---

* Augustine, *The Retractions,* trans. M. Inez Bogan, R.S.M., The fathers of
the Church (Baltimore: Catholic University of America Press, 1968), 52.

endless Native peoples on all continents and isolated islands for millennia just throwaways or dress rehearsals for "us"? Is God really that ineffective, boring, and stingy? Does the Almighty One operate from a scarcity model of love and forgiveness? Did the Divinity need to wait for Ethnic Orthodox, Roman Catholics, European Protestants, and American Evangelicals to appear before the divine love affair could begin? I cannot imagine!

Creation exists first of all for its own good sake; second to show forth God's goodness, diversity, and beneficence; and then for humans' appropriate use. Our small, scarcity-based worldview is the real aberration here, and I believe it has largely contributed to the rise of atheism and the "practical atheism" that is the actual operative religion of most Western countries today. The God we've been presenting people with is just too small and too stingy for a big-hearted person to trust or to love back.

Great Love and Great Suffering

You might wonder how, exactly, primitive peoples and pre-Christian civilizations could've had access to God. I believe it was through the universal and normal transformative journeys of *great love and great suffering*,* which all individuals have undergone from the beginnings of the human race. Only great love and great suffering are strong enough to take away our imperial ego's protections and open us to authentic experiences of transcendence. The Christ, especially when twinned with Jesus, is a clear message about *universal love and necessary suffering as the divine pattern*—starting with the three persons of the Trinity, where *God is said to be both endlessly outpouring and self-emptying.* Like three revolving buckets on a wa-

---

*   Rohr, *The Naked Now,* ch. 16.

terwheel, this process keeps the Flow flowing eternally—inside and outside of God, and in one positive direction.

Just because you do not have the right word for God does not mean you are not having the right experience. From the beginning, YHWH let the Jewish people know that no right word would ever contain God's infinite mystery. The God of Israel's message seems to be, "I am not going to give you any control over me, or else your need for control will soon extend to everything else." Controlling people try to control people, and they do the same with God—but loving anything always means a certain giving up of control. *You tend to create a God who is just like you—whereas it was supposed to be the other way around.* Did it ever strike you that God gives up control more than anybody in the universe? God hardly ever holds on to control, if the truth be told. We do. And God allows this every day in every way. God is so free.

Any kind of authentic God experience will usually feel like love or suffering, or both. It will connect you to Full Reality at ever-new breadths, and depths "until God will be all in all" (1 Corinthians 15:28). Our circles of belonging tend to either expand or constrict as life goes on. (At least that is what I've observed through working with people as a counselor, spiritual director, and confessor.) Our patterns of relating, once set, determine the trajectories for our whole lives. If we are inherently skeptical and suspicious, the focus narrows. If we are hopeful and trusting, the focus continues to expand.

Let me repeat again a point that has been so clarifying and foundational for me: *The proof that you are a Christian is that you can see Christ everywhere else.* This is what we saw in Caryll House- lander's experience on the train, and in Jesus when he pointed to divinity in "the least of the brothers and sisters" (Matthew 25:40) and even in the so-called bad thief who was crucified next to him (Luke 23:43). Authentic God experience always expands your seeing and never constricts it. What else would be worthy of God? *In God you do not include less and less; you always see and love more and more.* The more you transcend your small ego, the more you can include. "Unless the single grain of wheat dies, it remains just a single grain. But if it does, it will bear much fruit," Jesus Christ says (John 12:24).

When you look your dog in the face, for example, as I often looked at my black Labrador, Venus, I truly believe you are seeing another incarnation of the Divine Presence, the Christ. When you look at any other person, a flower, a honeybee, a mountain—anything—you are seeing the incarnation of God's love for you and the universe you call home.

Pause to focus on an incarnation of God's love apparent near you right now. You must risk it!

I hope a larger understanding is dawning for you. *Anything that draws you out of yourself in a positive way—for all practical purposes—is operating as God for you at that moment.* How else can the journey begin? How else are you drawn forward, now not by idle beliefs but by inner aliveness? God needs something to seduce you out and beyond yourself, so God uses three things in particular: goodness, truth, and beauty. All three have the capacity to draw us into an experience of union.

You cannot think your way into this kind of radiant, expansive seeing. You must be caught in a relationship of love and awe now and then, and it often comes slowly, through osmosis, imitation, resonance, contemplation, and mirroring. The Christ is always given freely, tossed like a baton from the other side. Our only part in the process is to reach out and catch it every now and then.

For Paul and for ordinary mystics like you and me, the kind of seeing I'm describing is a relational and reciprocal experience, in which we find God simultaneously in ourselves and in the outer world beyond ourselves. I doubt if there is any other way. Presence is never self-generated, but always a gift from another, and faith is always relational at the core. Divine seeing cannot be done alone, but only as one consciousness interfaces with another, and the two parties volley back and forth, meeting *subject to subject*. Presence must be offered and given, evoked and received. It can happen in a physical gesture, a quiet word or smile, a meal shared with someone we care for, where we are suddenly enlivened by a force larger than the two of us.

It is so important to taste, touch, and trust such moments. Words and complex rituals almost get in the way at this point. All you can really do is return such Presence with your own presence. Nothing to believe here at all. Just learn to trust and draw forth your own deepest experience, and you will know the Christ all day every day—before and after you ever go to any kind of religious service. Church, temple, and mosque will start to make sense on whole new levels—and at the same time, church, temple, and mosque will become totally boring and unnecessary. I promise you both will be true, because you are already fully accepted and fully accepting.

4

Original Goodness

Earth's crammed with heaven,
And every common bush afire with God;
But only he who sees takes off his shoes . . .
—Elizabeth Barrett Browning, *Aurora Leigh*

In the backyard of our Center for Action and Contemplation in New Mexico, a massive 150-year-old Rio Grande cottonwood tree spreads its gnarled limbs over the lawn. New visitors are drawn to it immediately, standing in its shade, looking upward into its mighty boughs. An arborist once told us that the tree might have a mutation that causes the huge trunks to make such circuitous turns and twists. One wonders how it stands so firmly, yet the cottonwood is easily the finest work of art that we have at the center, and its asymmetrical beauty makes it a perfect specimen for one of our organization's core messages: *Divine perfection is precisely the ability to include what seems like imperfection.* Before we come inside to pray, work, or teach any theology, its giant presence has already spoken a silent sermon over us.

Have you ever had an encounter like this in nature? Perhaps for you, it occurred at a lake or by the seashore, hiking in the mountains, in a garden listening to a mourning dove, even at a busy street corner. I am convinced that when received, such innate theology grows us, expands us, and enlightens us almost effortlessly. All other God talk seems artificial and heady in comparison.

Native religions largely got this, as did some scriptures. (See Daniel 3:57–82, or Psalms 98, 104, and 148.) In Job 12:7–10, and most of Job 38–39, Yahweh praises many strange animals and elements for their inherently available wisdom—the "pent up sea," the "wild ass," the "ostrich's wing"—reminding the human that he or she is part of a much greater ecosystem, which offers lessons in all directions. "Is it by your wisdom," God asks, "that the hawk soars, and spreads its wings to the south?" The obvious answer is no.

God is not bound by the human presumption that we are the center of everything, and creation did not actually demand or need Jesus (or *us,* for that matter) to confer additional sacredness upon it. From the first moment of the Big Bang, nature was revealing the glory and goodness of the Divine Presence; it must be seen as a gratuitous gift and not a necessity. Jesus came to live in its midst, and enjoy life in all its natural variations, and thus be our model and exemplar. *Jesus is the gift that honored the gift,* you might say.

Strangely, many Christians today limit God's provident care to humans, and very few of them at that. How different we are from Jesus, who extended the divine generosity to sparrows, lilies, ravens, donkeys, the grasses of the fields (Luke 12:22), and even "the hairs of the head" (Matthew 10:29). No stingy God here! (Although he did neglect the hairs of *my* head.) But what stinginess on our side made us limit God's concern—even eternal concern—to just ourselves? And how can we imagine God as caring about us if God does not care about everything else too? If God chooses and doles out his care, we are always insecure and unsure whether we are among the lucky recipients. But once we become aware of the generous, creative Presence that exists in all things natural, we can receive it as the inner Source of all dignity and worthiness. Dignity is not doled out to the worthy. It grounds the inherent worthiness of things in their very nature and existence.

The Great Chain of Being

St. Bonaventure (1221–1274) taught that *to work up to loving God, start by loving the very humblest and simplest things, and then move up from there.* "Let us place our first step in the ascent at the bottom, presenting to ourselves the whole material world as a mirror, through which we may pass over to God, who is the Supreme Craftsman," he wrote. And further, "The Creator's supreme power, wisdom and benevolence shine forth through all created things."*

I encourage you to apply this spiritual insight quite literally. Don't start by trying to love God, or even people; love rocks and elements first, move to trees, then animals, and then humans. Angels will soon seem like a real possibility, and God is then just a short leap away. It works. In fact, it might be the only way to love, because *how you do anything is how you do everything.* As John's First Letter says, quite directly, "Anyone who says he loves God and hates his brother [or sister] is a liar" (4:20). In the end, either you love everything or there is reason to doubt that you love anything. This one love and one loveliness was described by many medieval theologians and others as the "Great Chain of Being." The message

---

* Bonaventure, *The Soul's Journey to God* 1, 9–10 (New York: Paulist Press, 1978), 63.

was that if you failed to recognize the Presence in any one link of the chain, the whole sacred universe would fall apart. It really was "all or nothing."

God did not just start talking to us with the Bible or the church or the prophets. Do we really think that God had nothing at all to say for 13.7 billion years, and started speaking only in the latest nanosecond of geological time? Did all history prior to our sacred texts provide no basis for truth or authority? Of course not. The radiance of the Divine Presence has been glowing and expanding since the beginning of time, before there were any human eyes to see or know about it. But in the mid-nineteenth century, grasping for the certitude and authority the church was quickly losing in the face of rationalism and scientism, Catholics declared the Pope to be "infallible," and Evangelicals decided the Bible was "inerrant," despite the fact that we had gotten along for most of eighteen hundred years without either belief. In fact, these claims would have seemed idolatrous to most early Christians.

Creation—be it planets, plants, or pandas—was not just a warm-up act for the human story or the Bible. The natural world is its own good and sufficient story, if we can only learn to see it with humility and love. That takes contemplative practice, stopping our busy and superficial minds long enough to see the beauty, allow the truth, and protect the inherent goodness of what it is—whether it profits me, pleases me or not.

Every gift of food and water, every act of simple kindness, every ray of sunshine, every mammal caring for her young, all of it emerged from this original and intrinsically good creation. Humans were meant to know and enjoy this ever-present reality—a reality we too often fail to praise, or maybe worse, ignore and take for granted. As described in Genesis, the creation unfolds over six days, implying a developmental understanding of growth. Only the seventh day has no motion of it. The divine pattern is set: Doing must be balanced out by not-doing, in the Jewish tradition called the "Sabbath Rest." *All contemplation reflects a seventh-day choice and experience, relying on grace instead of effort.* Full growth implies timing and staging, acting and waiting, working and not working.

All the other sentient beings also do their little things, take their places in the cycle of life and death, mirroring the eternal self-emptying and eternal infilling of God, and somehow trusting it all—as did my dog Venus when she gazed at me, then looked straight ahead and humbly lowered her nose to the ground as we put her to sleep. Animals fear attack, of course, but they do not suffer the fear of death. Whereas many have said that the fear and avoidance of death is the one absolute in every human life.

If we can recognize that we belong to such a rhythm and ecosystem, and intentionally rejoice in it, we can begin to find our place in the universe. We will begin to see, as did Elizabeth Barrett Browning, that *Earth's crammed with heaven, And every common bush afire with God.*

Original Goodness, Not Original Sin

The true and essential work of all religion is to help us recognize and recover the divine image in everything. It is to mirror things correctly, deeply, and fully until all things know who they are. A mirror by its nature reflects impartially, equally, effortlessly, spontaneously, and endlessly. It does not produce the image, nor does it filter the image according to its perceptions or preferences. Authentic mirroring can only call forth what is already there.

But we can enlarge this idea of mirroring to give us another way to understand our key themes in this book. For example, there is a divine mirror that might be called the very "Mind of Christ." The Christ mirror fully knows and loves us from all eternity, and reflects that image back to us. I cannot logically prove this to you, but I do know that people who live inside of this resonance are both happy and healthy. Those who do not resonate and reciprocate with things around them only grow in loneliness and alienation, and invariably tend toward violence in some form, if only toward themselves.

Do you then also see the lovely significance of John's statement "It is not because you do not know the truth that I write to you, but because you know it already" (1 John 1:21)? He is talking about *an implanted knowing* in each of us—an inner mirror, if you will. Today, many would just call it "consciousness," and poets and musicians might call it the "soul." The prophet Jeremiah would call it "the Law written in your heart" (31:33), while Christians would call it the "Indwelling Holy Spirit." For me, these terms are largely interchangeable, approaching the same theme from different backgrounds and expectations.

In that same letter, John puts it quite directly: "My dear people, we are *already* the children of God, and what we are to be in the future is still to be revealed, and when it is revealed—all we will know is that we are like God, for we shall finally see God as he really is!" (3:2). And who is this God that we will finally see? It is somehow *Being Itself,* for God is the one, according to Paul, "in whom we live and move and have our [own] being, as indeed some of your own writers have said 'We are all his children'" (Acts 17:28).

Our inherent "likeness to God" depends upon the objective connection given by God equally to all creatures, each of whom carries the divine DNA in a unique way. Owen Barfield called this phenomenon "original participation." I would also call it "original blessing" or "original innocence" ("unwoundedness").*

Whatever you call it, the "image of God" is absolute and un-

---

* Owen Barfield, *Saving the Appearances* (Middletown, CT: Wesleyan University Press, 1988), ch. 6.

changing. There is nothing humans can do to increase or decrease it. And it is not ours to decide who has it or does not have it, which has been most of our problem up to now. It is pure and total gift, given equally to all.

But this picture was complicated when the concept of *original sin* entered the Christian mind.

In this idea—first put forth by Augustine in the fifth century, but never mentioned in the Bible—we emphasized that human beings were born into "sin" because Adam and Eve "offended God" by eating from the "tree of the knowledge of good and evil." As punishment, God cast them out of the Garden of Eden. This strange concept of original sin does not match the way we usually think of sin, which is normally a matter of personal responsibility and culpability. Yet original sin wasn't something we did at all; it was something that was done *to us* (passed down from Adam and Eve). So we got off to a bad start.

By contrast, most of the world's great religions start with some sense of primal goodness in their creation stories. The Judeo-Christian tradition beautifully succeeded at this, with the Genesis record telling us that God called creation "good" five times in Genesis 1:10–22, and even "very good" in 1:31. The initial metaphor for creation was a garden, which is inherently positive, beautiful, growth-oriented, a place to be "cultivated and cared for" (2:15), where humans could walk naked and without shame.

But after Augustine, most Christian theologies shifted from the positive vision of Genesis 1 to the darker vision of Genesis 3—the so-called fall, or what I am calling the "problem." Instead of embracing God's master plan for humanity and creation—what we Franciscans still call the "Primacy of Christ"—Christians shrunk our image of both Jesus and Christ, and our "Savior" became a mere Johnny-come-lately "answer" to the problem of sin, a problem that we had largely created ourselves. That's a very limited role for Jesus.

His *death* instead of his *life* was defined as saving us! This is no small point. The shift in what we valued often allowed us to avoid Jesus's actual life and teaching because all we needed was the sacrificial event of his death. Jesus became a mere mop-up exercise for sin, and sin management has dominated the entire religious story line and agenda to this day. This is no exaggeration.

In one way, the doctrine of "original sin" *was* good and helpful in that it taught us *not to be surprised at the frailty and woundedness that we all carry.* Just as goodness is inherent and shared, so it seems with evil. And this is, in fact, a very merciful teaching. Knowledge of our shared wound ought to free us from the burden of unnecessary—and individual—guilt or shame, and help us to be forgiving and compassionate with ourselves and with one another. (There is usually a bright side to every poor theological formulation, if we are willing to look for it.)

Yet historically, the teaching of original sin started us off on the wrong foot—*with a no instead of a yes, with a mistrust instead of a trust.* We have spent centuries trying to solve the "problem" that we're told is at the heart of our humanity. But if you start with a problem, you tend to never get beyond that mind-set.

From Augustine's theological *no,* the hole only got deeper. Martin Luther portrayed humans as a "pile of manure," John Calvin instituted his now-infamous doctrine of "total depravity," and poor Jonathan Edwards famously condemned New Englanders as "sinners in the hands of an angry God." No wonder Christians are accused of having a negative anthropology!

The theology of mistrust and suspicion has manifested itself in all kinds of misguided notions: a world always in competition with itself; a mechanical and magical understanding of baptism; fiery notions of hell; systems of rewards and punishments, shaming and exclusion of all wounded individuals (variously defined in each century); beliefs in the superiority of skin color, ethnicity, or nation.

All of this was done in the name of the one who said that he did not come "for the righteous" or the "virtuous," but for "sinners" (Luke 15:1–7, Mark 2:17, Luke 5:32), and to give us "life, and life abundantly" (John 10:10). This will never work, and it never did!

When we start with a theology of sin management administered by a too-often elite clergy, we end up with a schizophrenic religion. We end up with a Jesus who was merciful while on earth, but who punishes in the next world. Who forgives here but not later. God in this picture seems whimsical and untrustworthy even to the casual observer. It may be scary for Christians to admit these outcomes to ourselves, but we must. I believe this is a key reason why people do not so much react against the Christian story line, like they used to; instead, they simply refuse to take it seriously.

To begin climbing out of the hole of original sin, we must start with a positive and generous cosmic vision. Generosity tends to feed on itself. *I have never met a truly compassionate or loving human being who did not have a foundational and even deep trust in the inherent goodness of human nature.*

The Christian story line must start with a positive and over-arching vision for humanity and for history, or it will never get beyond the primitive, exclusionary, and fear-based stages of most early human development. We are ready for a major course correction.

Holding on to a Positive Vision

Brain studies have shown that we may be hardwired to focus on problems at the expense of a positive vision. The human brain wraps around fear and problems like Velcro. We dwell on bad experiences long after the fact, and spend vast amounts of energy antici-pating what might go wrong in the future. Conversely, positivity and gratitude and simple happiness slide away like cheese on hot Teflon.

Studies like the ones done by the neuroscientist Rick Hanson show that we must consciously hold on to a positive thought or feeling for a minimum of fifteen seconds before it leaves any imprint in the neurons. The whole dynamic, in fact, is called the Velcro/Teflon theory of the mind. We are more attracted to the problem than to the solution, you might say.*

I encourage you not to simply take me at my word. Watch your own brain and emotions. You will quickly see there is a toxic attraction to the "negative," whether it's a situation at work, a bit of incriminating gossip you overheard, or a sad development in the life of a friend. True freedom from this tendency is exceedingly rare, since we are ruled by automatic responses most of the time. The only way, then, to increase authentic spirituality is to *deliberately practice* actually enjoying a positive response and a grateful heart. And the benefits are very real. By following through on conscious choices, we can rewire our responses toward love, trust, and patience. Neuroscience calls this *"neuroplasticity."* This is how we increase our bandwidth of freedom, and it is surely the heartbeat of any authentic spirituality.

Most of us know that we can't afford to walk around fearing, hating, dismissing, and denying all possible threats and all otherness. But few of us were given practical teaching in how to avoid this. It is interesting that Jesus emphasized the absolute centrality of inner motivation and intention more than outer behavior, spending almost half of the Sermon on the Mount on this subject (see Matthew 5:20–6:18). We must—yes, *must*—make a daily and even hourly choice to focus on the good, the true, and the beautiful. A wonderful description of this act of the will is found in Philippians 4:4–9, where Paul writes, "Rejoice in the Lord *always* [italics added]." If you're

* Rick Hanson, *Hardwiring Happiness* (New York: Harmony Books, 2013), xxvi.

tempted to write this off as idyllic "positive thinking," remember that Paul wrote this letter while literally in chains (1:17). How did he pull this off? You might call it "mind control." Many of us just call it "contemplation."

So how do we first see and then practice this "Original Goodness"?

Paul again gives us an answer. He says, "There are only three things that last, faith, hope, and love" (1 Corinthians 13:13). In Catholic theology we called these three essential attitudes the "theological virtues," because they were a "participation in the very life of God"—given freely by God, or "infused" into us at our very conception. In this understanding, faith, hope, and love are far more defining of the human person than the "moral virtues," the various good behaviors we learn as we grow older. This is why I cannot abandon an Orthodox or Catholic worldview. For all of their poor formulations, they still offer humanity a foundationally *positive anthropology* (even though many individuals never learn about it because of poor catechesis!), and not just a moral worthiness contest, which is always unstable and insecure.

From the very beginning, faith, hope, and love are planted deep within our nature—indeed they *are* our very nature (Romans 5:5, 8:14–17). *The Christian life is simply a matter of becoming who we already are* (1 John 3:1–2, 2 Peter 1:3–4). But we have to awaken, allow, and advance this core identity by saying a conscious yes to it and drawing upon it as a reliable and Absolute Source.* Again, *image* must become *likeness*. And even a good theology will have a hard time making up for a bad anthropology. If the human person is a "pile of manure," even the "snow of Christ" only covers it and does not undo it.

But our saying yes to such implanted faith, hope, and love plays

---

* I wrote about this concept at greater length in my book *Immortal Diamond*.

a crucial role in the divine equation; human freedom matters. Mary's yes seemed to be essential to the event of incarnation (Luke 1:38). God does not come uninvited. God and grace cannot enter without an opening from our side, or we would be mere robots. God does not want robots, but lovers who freely choose to love in return for love. And toward that supreme end, God seems quite willing to wait, cajole, and entice.

In other words, *we matter*. We do have to choose to trust reality and even our physicality, which is to finally trust ourselves. Our readiness to *not* trust ourselves is surely one of our recurring sins. Yet so many sermons tell us to *never* trust ourselves, to *only* trust God. That is far too dualistic. How can a person who does not trust himself know how to trust at all? Trust, like love, is of one piece. (By the way, at this point in history, *"trust"* is probably a much more helpful and descriptive word than "faith," a notion that has become far too misused, intellectualized, and even banal.)

In the practical order, we find our Original Goodness when we can discover and own these three attitudes or virtues deeply planted within us:

A trust in inner coherence itself. "It all means something!"
   (Faith)
A trust that this coherence is positive and going somewhere good
   (Hope)
A trust that this coherence includes me and even defines me
   (Love)

This is the soul's foundation. That we are capable of such trust and surrender is the objective basis for human goodness and holiness, and it almost needs to be rechosen day by day lest we continue to slide toward cynicism, victim playing and making, and a common self-pity. No philosophy or government, no law or reason, can fully offer or promise us this attitude, but the Gospel can and does. Healthy religion has the power to offer us a compelling and attractive foundation for human goodness and dignity, and show us ways to build on that foundation.

In every age and culture, we have seen regressions toward racism, sexism, homophobia, militarism, lookism, and classism. This pattern tells me that unless we see dignity as being given universally, objectively, and from the beginning by God, humans will constantly think it is up to us to decide. But this tragic history demonstrates that one group cannot be trusted to portion out worthiness and dignity to another. Our criteria tend to be self-referential and thus highly prejudiced, and the powerless and the disadvantaged always lose out. Even America's glorious Declaration of Independence—which states that "[all people] are endowed by their Creator with certain unalienable rights"—has not empowered the white majority to apportion those rights immediately and equally up to now.

For the planet and for all living beings to move forward, we can rely on nothing less than *an inherent original goodness and a universally shared dignity*. Only then can we build, because the foundation is strong, and is itself good. Surely this is what Jesus meant when he told us to "dig and dig deep, and build your house on rock" (Luke 6:48). When you start with *yes* (or a positive vision), you more likely proceed with generosity and hope, and you have a much greater chance of ending with an even bigger yes. To try to build on *no* is, in the imagery of Jesus, to "build on sand."

If our postmodern world seems highly subject to cynicism, skepticism, and what it does *not* believe in, if we now live in a post-truth America, then we "believers" must take at least partial responsibility for aiming our culture in this sad direction. *The best criticism of the bad is still the practice of the better.* Oppositional energy only creates more of the same. All problem solving must first be guided by a positive and overarching vision.

We must reclaim the Christian project, building from the true starting point of Original Goodness. We must reclaim Jesus as an inclusive Savior instead of an exclusionary Judge, as a Christ who holds history together as the cosmic Alpha and Omega. Then, both history and the individual can live inside of a collective safety and an assured success. Some would call this the very shape of salvation.

5

Love Is the Meaning

Know it well, love is its meaning.
Who reveals this to you? Love.
What does he reveal? Love. Why? For Love.
Remain in this and you will know more of the same.

—Lady Julian of Norwich, *Showings*

For Pierre Teilhard de Chardin (1881–1955), a French Jesuit priest who trained as a paleontologist and geologist, love is the very physical structure of the Universe. That is a very daring statement, especially for a scientist to make. But for Teilhard, gravity, atomic bonding, orbits, cycles, photosynthesis, ecosystems, force fields, electromagnetic fields, sexuality, human friendship, animal instinct, and evolution all reveal an energy that is attracting all things and beings to one another, in a movement toward ever greater complexity and diversity—and yet ironically also toward unification at ever deeper levels. This energy is quite simply *love under many different forms.* (You can use other words if they work better for you.)

In this chapter, I want to talk about this foundational force of love, and how a Jesus who is also Christ allows us to see it and participate in it ever more fully.

What Love Tells Us About God

Love, which might be called the attraction of all things toward all things, is a universal language and underlying energy that keeps showing itself despite our best efforts to resist it. It is so simple that it is hard to teach in words, yet we all know it when we see it. After all, there is not a Native, Hindu, Buddhist, Jewish, Islamic, or Christian way of loving. There is not a Methodist, Lutheran, or Orthodox way of running a soup kitchen. There is not a gay or straight way of being faithful, nor a Black or Caucasian way of hoping. We all know positive flow when we see it, and we all know resistance and coldness when we feel it. All the rest are mere labels.

When we are truly "in love," we move out of our small, individual selves to unite with another, whether in companionship, simple friendship, marriage, or any other trustful relationship. Have you ever deliberately befriended a person standing alone at a party? Perhaps someone who was in no way attractive to you, or with whom you shared no common interests? That would be a small but real example of divine love flowing. Don't dismiss it as insignificant. That is how the flow starts, even if the encounter doesn't change anyone's life on the spot. To move beyond our small-minded uniformity, we have to extend ourselves outward, which our egos always find a threat, because it means giving up our separation, superiority, and control.

Men seem to have an especially difficult time at this. I have had the pleasure of presiding at many weddings over the years. Three different times, as I prepared the couple to exchange their vows, the groom actually fainted and fell to the ground. But I have never seen the bride faint. To the well-protected and boundaried male ego, there are few greater threats than the words "till death do us part." (I am sure women have their blockages too.) That may be why so many cultures created initiation rites to teach men how to trust, let go, and surrender.*

Love is a paradox. It often involves making a clear decision, but at its heart, it is not a matter of mind or willpower but *a flow of energy willingly allowed and exchanged, without requiring payment in return.* Divine love is, of course, the template and model for such human love, and yet human love is the necessary school for any encounter with divine love. If you've never experienced human love—to the point of sacrifice and forgiveness and generosity—it will be very hard for you to access, imagine, or even experience God's kind of love. Conversely, if you have never let God love you in the deep and subtle ways that God does, you will not know how to love another human in the deepest ways of which you are capable.

Love is constantly creating future possibilities for the good of all concerned—even, and especially, when things go wrong. Love allows and accommodates everything in human experience, both the good and the bad, and *nothing else can really do this.* Nothing. Love flows unstoppably downward, around every obstacle—like water. Love and water seek not the higher place but always the lower. That's why forgiveness is often the most powerful display of love in action. When we forgive, we acknowledge that there is, in fact, something to forgive—a mistake, an offense, an error—but instead of reverting to survival mode, we release the offending party from any need for punishment or recrimination. In so doing, we bear

---

* I wrote about this at length in *Adam's Return* (New York: Crossroad, 2004).

witness to the Ever Risen and Always Loving Christ, who is always "going ahead of you into Galilee, and that is where you will see him" (Matthew 28:7). Un-forgiveness lives in a repetitive past, which it cannot let go of. But forgiveness is a *largeness of soul,* without which there is no future or creative action—only the repetition of old story lines, remembered hurts, and ever-increasing claims of victimhood for all concerned.

An eagerness and readiness to love is the ultimate freedom and future. When you've been included in the spaciousness of divine love, there is just no room for human punishment, vengeance, rash judgment, or calls for retribution. We certainly see none of this small-mindedness in the Risen Christ after his own rejection, betrayal, and cruel death; we don't see it even from his inner circle, or in the whole New Testament. I really cannot imagine a larger and more spacious way to live. Jesus's death and resurrection event was a game changer for history, and it is no surprise that we date our calendar from his lifetime.

The Crucified and Risen Christ uses the mistakes of the past to create a positive future, a future of redemption instead of retribution. He does not eliminate or punish the mistakes. He uses them for transformative purposes.

People formed by such love are indestructible.

Forgiveness might just be the very best description of what God's goodness engenders in humanity.

Waking Up

Religion, at its best, helps people to bring this foundational divine love into ever-increasing consciousness. In other words, it's more about waking up than about cleaning up. Early-stage religion tends to focus on cleaning up, which is to say, determining who meets the requirements for moral behavior and religious belief. But Jesus threw a wrench into this whole machinery by refusing to enforce or even bother with what he considered secondary issues like the Sabbath, ritual laws, purity codes, membership requirements, debt codes, on and on. He saw they were only "human commandments," which far too often took the place of love. (See especially Matthew 15:3, 6–9.) Or as he puts it in another place, "You hypocrites, you pay your tithes . . . and neglect the weightier matters of the law: justice, mercy, and good faith" (Matthew 23:23). Cleaning up is a result of waking up, but most of us put the cart before the horse.

It's no wonder his fellow Jews had to kill Jesus, just as many Catholics would love to eliminate Pope Francis today. Once you *wake up,* as Jesus and Pope Francis have, you know that cleaning up is a constant process that comes on different timetables for different people, around many different issues, and for very different motivations. This is why love and growth demand discernment, not enforcement. When it comes to actual soul work, most attempts at policing and conforming are largely useless. It took me most of my life as a confessor, counselor, and spiritual director to be honest and truly helpful with people about this.* Mere obedience is far too often a detour around actual love. Obedience is usually about cleaning up, love is about waking up.

At this point, at least in the United States, it appears that our cultural meaning has pretty much shrunk down to this: *It is all about winning.* Then, once you win, it becomes all about consuming. I can discern no other underlying philosophy in the practical order of American life today. Of itself, such a worldview cannot feed the soul very well or very long, much less provide meaning and encouragement, or engender love or community.

For insight into a more life-giving worldview, we can look to

---

* Richard Rohr, *Falling Upward* (San Francisco: Jossey-Bass, 2011).

scripture and wise saints such as Julian of Norwich (1342–1416), whose statement that "love is its meaning" opens this chapter. After years of counseling both religious and nonreligious people, it seems to me that most humans need a love object (which will then become a subject!) to keep themselves both sane and happy. That love object becomes our "North Star," serving as our moral compass and our reason to keep putting one foot in front of the other in a happy and hopeful way. All of us need someone or something to connect our hearts with our heads. Love grounds us by creating focus, direction, motivation, even joy—and if we don't find these things in love, we usually will try to find them in hate. Do you see the consequences of this unmet need in our population today? I do.

One place where I often see a positive focus and purpose is in the hardworking happiness of young mothers and fathers. Their new child becomes their one North Star, and they know very clearly why they are waking up each morning. This is the God Instinct, which we might just call the "need to adore." It is the need for one overarching focus, direction, and purpose in life, or what the Hebrew Scriptures describe as "one God before you" (Exodus 20:3). Parenting and family are the primary school for the love instinct, and always will be. They serve as the basic container, in which the soul, the heart, the body, and even the mind can flourish. Thus we leave one family only to create another. When I worked in the jail for fourteen years, I saw that the inmates even tried to create family there. Many insisted on calling me "Father" and their best friends "Bro"! The need for secure grounding and mirroring never stops.

Humans seem to want, even need something (or someone) that we can give ourselves to totally, something that focuses and gathers our affections. We need at least one place where we can "kneel and kiss the ground," as Rumi, the Sufi poet and mystic, put it. Or as the French friar Eloi Leclerc (1921–2016) beautifully paraphrased Francis: "If we knew how to *adore*, then nothing could truly disturb our peace. We would travel through the world with the tranquility of the *great rivers*. But only if we know how to *adore*."* Of course, adoration is finally the response to something Perfect. But the genius of love is that it teaches us how to give ourselves to imperfect things too. *Love, you might say, is the training ground for adoration.*

"Love Made Me Do It!"

In some ways, the object of our affection is arbitrary. It can begin as a love of golf, a clean house, your cat; or a desire to cultivate a certain reputation for yourself. Granted, the largeness of the object will eventually determine the largeness of the love, but God will use anything to get you started, focused, and flowing. Only a very few actually start this journey with God as the object. And that is fully to be expected. *God is not in competition with reality, but in full cooperation with it.* All human loves, passions, and preoccupations can prime the pump, and only in time do most of us discover the first and final Source of those loves. God is clearly humble and does not seem to care who or what gets the credit. Whatever elicits the flow for you—in that moment and encounter, that thing *is* God for you! I do not say that without theological foundation, because my Trinitarian faith says that God is Relationship Itself. The names of the three "persons" of the Trinity are not so important as the relationship between them. That's where all the power is at.

In the Gospel accounts of Jesus's healings, we find a striking lack of logic to who gets healed and who doesn't. In none of the accounts does the healing depend on the person's worthiness. Sometimes the recipients of healing do not ask for it themselves—Jesus has to

---

* Eloi Leclerc, *The Wisdom of the Poor One of Assisi,* trans. Marie-Louise Johnson (Pasadena, CA: Hope Publishing House, 1992), 72.

ask them if they even want to be healed (John 5:7). But somehow, across all of these accounts, Jesus is able to *complete the circuit* of divine electricity in certain people, healing them physically sometimes, but always spiritually. Don't mistake this as a *direct current* from Jesus to the healed person. Jesus consistently refuses to be characterized as a miracle worker, and he runs from both notoriety and fame. This is why, after healing someone, he never said, "My magic power did it. Now come join my religion!" Instead, he usually says something like "Your faith has saved you, now go in peace!" (Matthew 9:22, Mark 5:34, Luke 8:48). I think humans prefer magical religion, which keeps all the responsibility on God performing or not performing. Whereas mature and transformational religion asks *us* to participate, cooperate, and change. The divine dance is always a partnered two-step.

Jesus puts healed people back on themselves, never creating any kind of dependency or codependency on him that will keep them from their own empowerment. All people must learn to draw from their own Implanted Spirit, which is the only thing that will help them in the long run anyway. Jesus gives them the courage to trust their own "inner Christ"—and not just its outer manifestation in himself. Go reread the Gospels and see if that is not true!

You might say that the Eternal Christ is the symbolic "superconductor" of the Divine Energies into this world. Jesus ramps down the ohms so we can handle divine love and receive it through ordinary human mediums.

To complete the circuit of Divine Love, we often need a moment of awe, a person who evokes that electric conductivity, something we can deeply respect, or even call "Father" or "Mother" or "Lover" or just "beautiful." Only then do we find the courage and confidence to complete God's circuit from our side. This is why people know they do not fully choose love; they fall into it, allow it, and then receive its strong charge. The evidence that you are involved in this flow will often seem two-sided. *You are simultaneously losing control and finding it.*

When Peter tells Jesus with gushing enthusiasm, "You are the Christ, the Son of the Living God!" Jesus then tells him that "flesh and blood"—meaning human logic or effort from our side—cannot get you to this conclusion, but "My Father in heaven has revealed this to you" (Matthew 16:16–17).* Similarly, as I look at the things and people I have tried to love in my life, I would have to say, "They made me do it!" It was the inherent goodness, inner beauty, vulnerability, deep honesty, or generosity of spirit from the other side that drew me out of myself and toward them. In a very real sense, I did not initiate love toward them. Rather, it was taken from me! It was pulled out of me—by them.

Grace is just the natural loving flow of things when we allow it, instead of resisting it.

Sin is any cutting or limiting of that circuit. And we all sin now and then.

But an occasional power outage can help you appreciate how much you need unearned love and deeply rely upon it. Failure is part of the deal!

Moving in the Divine Two-Step

Let me offer a further quotation from Teilhard's *Divine Milieu,* remembering that humans do not tend to get invested in things unless those things somehow include them:

---

* See also Romans 8:28–29, where Paul says that it is "co-operators" who "become true images of his Son, so that Jesus might be the eldest of many brothers [and sisters]."

> God does not offer Himself to our finite beings as a thing all complete and ready to be embraced. For us, He is eternal discovery and eternal growth. The more we think we understand Him, the more he reveals himself as otherwise. The more we think we hold him, the further He withdraws, drawing us into the depths of himself.*

This so fits my own experience of God. The divine-human love affair really is a reciprocal dance. Sometimes, in order for us to step forward, the other partner must step a bit away. The withdrawal is only for a moment, and its purpose is to pull us toward him or her—but it doesn't feel like that in the moment. It feels like our partner is retreating. Or it just feels like suffering.

God creates the pullback too, "hiding his face" as it was called by so many mystics and Scriptures. God creates a vacuum that God alone can fill. Then God waits to see if we will trust our God partner to eventually fill the space in us, which now has grown even more spacious and receptive. This is the central theme of darkness, necessary doubt, or what the mystics called "God withdrawing his love." They knew that what feels like suffering, depression, uselessness—moments when God has withdrawn—these moments are often deep acts of trust and invitation to intimacy on God's part. (That this is so poorly understood was revealed when the world was shocked to discover that Mother Teresa had many years of darkness and what looked to the secular world like depression. It was anything but.)

I must be honest with you here about my own life. For the last ten years I have had little spiritual "feeling," neither consolation nor desolation. Most days, I've had to simply choose to believe, to love,

---

* Pierre Teilhard de Chardin, *Divine Milieu* (New York: Harper & Row, 1965), 139.

and to trust. The simple kindness and gratitude of good people pro-
duces a momentary "good feeling" in me, but even this goodness I
do not know how to hold on to. It slides off my consciousness like
that cheese on a Teflon pan!

But God rewards me for letting him reward me.
This is the divine two-step that we call grace:
I am doing it, and yet I am not doing it;
It is being done unto me, and yet by me too.
Yet God always takes the lead in the dance, which we only recog-
nize over time.

What kind of God would only push from without, and never
draw from within? Yet this is precisely the one-sided God that most
of us were offered, and that much of the world has now rejected.

When we speak of Christ, we are speaking of an ever-growing
encounter, and never a fixed package that is all-complete and must
be accepted as is. On the inner journey of the soul we meet a God
who interacts with our deepest selves, who grows the person, allowing and forgiving mistakes. It is precisely this give-and-take, and
knowing there will be give-and-take, that makes God so real as a
Lover. God unfolds your personhood from within through a *constant increase in freedom—even freedom to fail.* Love cannot happen
in any other way. This is why Paul shouts in Galatians, "For freedom Christ has set us free!" (Galatians 5:1).

Remember again, *God loves you by becoming you,* taking your
side in the inner dialogue of self-accusation and defense. God loves
you by turning your mistakes into grace, by constantly giving you
back to yourself in a larger shape. God stands with you, and not
against you, when you are tempted to shame or self-hatred. If your
authority figures never did that for you, it can be hard to feel it or
trust it.* But you must experience this love at a cellular level at least

---

*   This certainly is not helped by the fact that threats and punishment were once. (Remember, the only thing that separates you from God is *the thought* that you are separate from God!)

Every attempt to describe any and every action, or seeming inaction, of God will always be relational, interpersonal, and loving—and totally inclusive of you. In light of the Christ Mystery, this unifying love by which the entire material world is governed, we learn that God can never be experienced apart from *your best interests being involved.* Hard to imagine, isn't it? Those who doubt it have never asked for it, or needed love enough to ask for it. Those who ask, always know and thus receive (Matthew 7:7). "If you, evil as you are, know how to give your children what is good, how much more will the heavenly Father give good things to those who ask him" (7:11). Human loves are the trial runs. Divine love is always the goal. But it can only build on all the stepping-stones of human relationships—and then it includes them all!

The receiving of love lets us know that there was indeed a Giver.

And freedom to even ask for love is the beginning of the receiving.

Thus Jesus can rightly say, "If you ask, you will receive" (Matthew 7:7–8).

To ask is to open the conduit from your side.

Your asking is only seconding the motion.

The first motion is always from God.

---

the rather universal method of parenting until very recently.

6

A Sacred Wholeness

*Truly, my life is one long hearkening unto myself and
unto others, and unto God.*

—Etty Hillesum, *An Interrupted Life*

Etty Hillesum, a young Jewish woman who was killed at Auschwitz
in 1943, provides all of us with an important example of a non-
Christian witness to the universal Christ Mystery. Before being
imprisoned by the Nazis, Etty had been a quite modern woman,
as unafraid of life, of her sexuality and other sensual pleasures, as
she finally was of death. Yet, although she wasn't a Christian, she
was highly spiritual in the best sense of that term. She was an utter
realist, devoid of self-pity, and with an almost impossible freedom
from need to blame, hate, or project her inner anxiety elsewhere.

Without desiring to patronize her, I would identify Etty as a person Karl Rahner would've called an "anonymous Christian," someone who unravels the underlying mystery of incarnation better than

most Christians I know. Such folks are much more common than Christians imagine, although they do not need that appellation.

As the Nazis began their campaign of genocide and Etty's future became more and more uncertain, she addressed God repeatedly in her diaries, regarding him not as an external savior, but as *a power she could nurture and feed inside of her.* She honored and loved this very power in his seeming powerlessness (which is the precise meaning of the crucified Jesus). Just listen to the power of these words to God:

> Alas, there doesn't seem to be much You Yourself can do about our circumstances, about our lives. Neither do I hold You responsible. You cannot help us, but we must help You and defend Your dwelling place inside us to the last.*

In another place, a letter to a close friend from the Westerbork transit camp not long before she was sent to Auschwitz, she writes from that foundational place of faith, hope, and love that I talked about in the last chapter:

> [In] spite of everything you always end up with the same conviction: life is good after all, it's not God's fault that things go awry sometimes, the cause lies in ourselves. And that's what stays with me, even now, even when I'm about to be packed off to Poland with my whole family.†

And, in yet another place, she incomprehensibly writes as if she is a different species of human being:

---

* Etty Hillesum, *Etty: The Letters and Diaries of Etty Hillesum, 1941–43* (Grand Rapids: William Eerdmans Publishing, 2002), 488.

† Ibid, 608.

Those two months behind barbed wire have been the two richest and most intense months of my life, in which my highest values were so deeply confirmed. I have learnt to love Westerbork.*

Reflections like these—especially considering the circumstances—make Etty a profound expression for us of complete wholeness, or what St. Bonaventure called the "coincidence of opposites." How does anyone achieve such a holding together of opposites—things like inner acceptance and outer resistance, intense suffering and perfect freedom, my little self and an infinite God, sensuality and intense spirituality, the need to blame somebody and the freedom to blame nobody? Etty Hillesum demonstrated this ability like few people I have ever studied. Either such people are the cutting edge of human consciousness and civilization, or they are mentally deranged. They surely far transcend any formal religion.

Etty Hillesum is but one example of another function of the Christ: a universally available "voice" that calls all things to *become whole and true to themselves.* God's two main tools in this direction, from every appearance, seem to be great love and great suffering—and often great love that *invariably leads* to great suffering.

The supreme irony of life is that this voice of Christ works through—and alongside of—what always seems like unwholeness and untruth! God insists on incorporating the seeming negative. There is no doubt that God allows suffering. In fact, *God seems to send us on the path toward our own wholeness not by eliminating the obstacles, but by making use of them.* Most of the novels, operas, and poems ever written seem to have this same message in one way or another, yet it still comes as a shock and a disappointment when we experience it in our own little lives. But apart from love and

---

* Ibid, 520.

suffering, both of which are always underserved, I see no other way that humans would recalibrate, reset, or change course. Why would we?

The Whole-Making Instinct

Carl Jung (1875–1961), the famous Swiss psychiatrist and psycho-analyst, was highly critical of his Christian heritage because he did not find much transformation—what he called "whole making"—in the Christians he knew. Instead, he saw a religious tradition that had become externally focused, moralistic, and ineffective in actu-ally changing people or cultures. His own father and five uncles were Swiss Reformed ministers, and Jung found them to be un-happy and unhealthy men. I am not sure what his exact evidence for this perception was, but clearly it was disillusioning to Jung. He did not want to end up like the religious men in his life.

Yet Jung was neither an atheist nor anti-Christian. He insisted that each of us has an inner "God Archetype," or what he termed the "whole-making instinct." The God Archetype is the part of you that drives you toward greater inclusivity by deep acceptance of the Real, the balancing of opposites, simple compassion toward the self, and the ability to recognize and forgive your own shadow side. For Jung, wholeness was not to be confused with any kind of supposed moral perfection, because such moralism is too tied up with ego and denial of the inner weakness that all of us must accept. I deeply agree with him.

In his critique of his father and uncles, Jung recognized that many humans had become reflections of the punitive God they worshiped. A forgiving God allows us to recognize the good in the supposed bad, and the bad in the supposed perfect or ideal. *Any view of God as tyrannical or punitive tragically keeps us from admitting these seeming contradictions.* It keeps us in denial about our true selves, and forces us to live on the surface of our own lives. If God is a shaming figure, then most of us naturally learn to deny, deflect, or pass on that shame to others. If God is torturer in chief, then a punitive and moralistic society is validated all the way down. We are back into problem-solving religion instead of healing and transformation.

Wholeness for Jung was about harmony and balancing, a holding operation more than an expelling operation. But he recognized that such consciousness was costly, because humans prefer to deal with the tensions of life by various forms of denial, moralizing, addiction, or projection. By the 1930s, Jung said there was so much repressed, denied, and projected shadow material in Europe, the supposedly Christian continent, that another Great War was almost inevitable. Tragically, his prediction ended up being fully correct.

I do not think Jung would have been exposed to my distinction between Jesus and Christ. More likely, he would have used the two words interchangeably, as have most people up to now. But if I read him correctly, his God Archetype can teach us something important about the Christ Mystery, and our participation in it. He understood that *the full journey towards wholeness must always include the negative experiences (the "cross") that we usually reject.* In that, Jung was more Christian than the critics who called him anti-Christian.

The Voice That Is Great Within Us

To follow their own paths to wholeness, both Etty Hillesum and Carl Jung trusted in and hearkened to the voice of God in their deepest Selves. Many educated and sophisticated people are not willing to submit to indirect, subversive, and intuitive knowing, which is probably why they rely far too much on external law and ritual behavior to achieve their spiritual purposes. They know nothing else that feels objective and solid. Intuitive truth, that inner whole-making instinct, just feels too much like *our own thoughts and feelings,* and most of us are not willing to call this "God," even when that voice prompts us toward compassion instead of hatred, forgiveness instead of resentment, generosity instead of stinginess, bigness instead of pettiness. But think about it: If the incarnation is true, then *of course* God speaks to you through your own thoughts! As Joan of Arc brilliantly replied when the judge accused her of being the victim of her own imagination, "How else would God speak to me?"

Many of us have been trained to write off these inner voices as mere emotion, religious conditioning, or psychological manipulation. Perhaps they sometimes are, but often they are *not.* God talk seems beneath the dignity of the modern and postmodern person. Ironically, this is half right. The inner voice so honored by Hillesum and Jung is experienced as the deepest and usually hidden self, where most of us do not go. It truly does speak at a level "beneath" rational consciousness, a place where only the humble—or the trained—know how to go.

At one point, Jung wrote, *"My pilgrim's progress has been to climb down a thousand ladders until I could finally reach out a hand of friendship to the little clod of earth that I am."** Jung, a supposed unbeliever, knew that any authentic God experience takes a lot of humility and a lot of honesty. The proud cannot know God because God is not proud, but infinitely humble. Remember, only like can know like! A combination of humility and patient seeking is the best spiritual practice of all.

---

* *C. G. Jung Letters, vol. 1,* selected and edited by Gerhard Adler (London: Routledge, 1972), 19, n. 8.

And this is where embracing the Christ Mystery becomes utterly practical. *Without the mediation of Christ, we will be tempted to overplay the distance and the distinction between God and humanity.* But because of the incarnation, the supernatural is forever embedded in the natural, making the very distinction false. How good is that? This is why saints like Augustine, Teresa of Avila, and Carl Jung seem to fully equate the discovery of their own souls with the very discovery of God. It takes much of our life, much lived experience, to trust and allow such a process. But when it comes, *it will feel like a calm and humble ability to quietly trust yourself and trust God at the same time.* Isn't that what we all want?

If you can trust and listen to this inner divine image, this whole-making instinct, or what I called in an earlier book your "True Self,"* you will be moving forward with your best, your largest, your kindest, your most inclusive self. (I should also add "your most *compassionately dissatisfied* self," because the soul's journey invites us to infinite depth that we can never fully plumb!) As Augustine says, "A temporal thing is loved before we have it, and it grows worthless when we gain it, for it does not satisfy the soul . . . but the eternal is more ardently loved the more it is acquired. . . . The soul will find the eternal even more valuable after once tasting it."† I am quite sure this is what drove Etty Hillesum ever deeper and ever forward, and allowed her to follow a very sensual, even sexual experience in the bedroom with prayers of adoration on the bathroom floor, all within the same half hour.

Spiritual satisfactions feed on themselves, grow by themselves, create wholeness, and are finally their own reward. Material satisfactions, while surely not bad, have a tendency to become addictive,

---

* Rohr, *Immortal Diamond.*

† Augustine, *On Christian Doctrine* 1. 38.42, in *Readings in Classic Rhetoric* (New York: Routledge, 2008), 184.

because instead of making you whole, they repeatedly remind you of how incomplete, needy, and empty you are. As alcoholics often say, your "addiction makes you need more and more of what is not working." Spiritual satisfactions will often be communicated to us in material, embodied, and ecstatic forms, however. Embodiment is good and necessary, so don't dismiss it too quickly as "the flesh." The difference is in how we encounter these forms. If we can be satisfied to enjoy them, observe them, participate in them, they give us ongoing joy. They are fingers pointing at the moon. But once we try to possess, capture, or "own" the moon, or any material thing, pulling it inside our own ego control, it is somehow polluted. Social scientists say that the excitement that surrounds the opening of a physical gift fades within a very few minutes.

In fact, far from consuming spiritual gifts for yourself alone, you must receive all words of God tenderly and subtly, so that you can speak them to others tenderly and with subtlety. I would even say that anything said with too much bravado, overassurance, or with any need to control or impress another, is *never* the voice of God within you. I hope I am not doing that here. If any thought feels too harsh, shaming, or diminishing of yourself or others, it is not likely the voice of God. Trust me on that. That is simply *your* voice. Why do humans so often presume the exact opposite—that shaming voices are always from God, and grace voices are always the imagination? That is a self-defeating ("demonic"?) path. Yet, as a confessor and a spiritual director, I can confirm that this broken logic is the general norm.

If something comes toward you with grace and can pass through you and toward others with grace, you can trust it as the voice of God.

Try doing this for yourself—maybe even out loud. It only comes with practice. One recent holy man who came to visit me put it this way, *"We must listen to what is supporting us. We must listen to what is encouraging us. We must listen to what is urging us. We must listen to what is alive in us.*" I personally was so trained *not* to trust those voices that I think I often did not hear the voice of God speaking to me, or what Abraham Lincoln called the "better angels of our nature." Yes, a narcissistic person can and will misuse such advice, but a genuine God lover will flourish inside such a dialogue. That is the risk that God takes—and we must take—for the sake of a fruitful love relationship with God. It takes so much courage and humility to trust the voice of God within. Mary fully personifies such trust in her momentous and free "Let It Be" to the Archangel Gabriel (Luke 1:38), and she was an uneducated teenage Jewish girl.

Most Christians have been taught to hate or confess our sin before we've even recognized its true shape. But if you nurture hatred toward yourself, it won't be long before it shows itself as hatred toward others. This is garden-variety Christianity, I am afraid, but it comes at a huge cost to history. *Unless religion leads us on a path to both depth and honesty, much religion is actually quite dangerous to the soul and to society.* In fact, *"fast-food religion" and the so-called prosperity gospel are some of the very best ways to actually avoid God—while talking about religion almost nonstop.*

We must learn how to recognize the positive flow and to distinguish it from the negative resistance within ourselves. It takes years, I think. *If a voice comes from accusation and leads to accusation, it is quite simply the voice of the "Accuser," which is the literal meaning of the biblical word "Satan."* Shaming, accusing, or blaming is simply not how God talks. It is how *we* talk. God is supremely nonviolent, and I have learned that from the saints and mystics that I have read and met and heard about. That many holy people cannot be wrong.

7

Going Somewhere Good

I have come to cast fire upon the earth,
and how I wish it were already blazing.

—Luke 12:49

Up to now, we've focused largely on describing a universal and deeper reality at the heart of all things. We have named this transcendent reality the Christ Mystery, which reveals itself in the incarnations of nature, the Jesus of history, and even you and me. This Christ passionately and relentlessly loves us in a highly personalized way, wooing us toward wholeness in a vocabulary unique to each soul.

In this chapter, we stand back to ask, *But where is this all going? If "Christ in you" is the starting point, what is the end goal for all of us, and—for that matter—the cosmos in its entirety?* Is our "late, great planet earth" really headed toward Armageddon? In these fractious, unmoored, and disillusioned times, I can hardly think of more relevant concerns.

To arrive at ultimate outcomes, I begin with the promise of change, and also the nature of change, which I describe later as moving from order to disorder and finally reorder (Appendix II).

The Inner Process of Change

Jesus's daring notion of casting fire upon the earth, cited in the epigraph, is one of my favorite metaphors. I love the image of fire, not for its seeming destructiveness, but as a natural symbol for transformation—literally, the changing of forms. Farmers, forestry workers, and Native peoples know that fire is a renewing force, even as it also can be destructive. We in the West tend to see it as merely destructive (which is probably why we did not understand the metaphors of hell or purgatory).

Jesus quite clearly believed in change. In fact, the first public word out of his mouth was the Greek imperative verb *metanoeite*, which literally translates as "change your mind" or "go beyond your mind" (Matthew 3:2, 4:17, and Mark 1:15). Unfortunately, in the fourth century, St. Jerome translated the word into Latin as *paenitentia* ("repent" or "do penance"), initiating a host of moralistic connotations that have colored Christians' understanding of the Gospels ever since. The word *metanoeite,* however, is talking about *a primal change of mind, worldview, or your way of processing*—and only by corollary about a specific change in behavior. The common misunderstanding puts the cart before the horse; we think we can change a few externals while our underlying worldview often remains fully narcissistic and self-referential.

This misunderstanding contributed to a puritanical, externalized, and largely static notion of the Christian message that has followed us to this day. Faith became about external requirements that could be enforced, punished, and rewarded, much more than an *actual change of heart and mind,* which Jesus describes as something that largely happens "in secret, where your Father who sees all that is done in secret can reward you" (Matthew 6:4, 6, 18). Jesus invariably emphasized *inner motivation and intention* in his moral teaching. He made religion about interior change and "purity of heart" (Matthew 5:8), rather than anything people can see, or anything that will produce any social payoff or punishment. This refines religion at the very point where it's most likely to become corrupt and manipulative.

The inner process of change is fundamental to everything, even our bodies. Think about it: What if the next wound to your body could never be healed? Having undergone several surgeries myself, I was consoled by the way my body always took care of itself over time. The miracle of healing came from the inside; all I had to do was wait and trust. In religion, though, many prefer magical, external, one-time transactions instead of the universal pattern of growth and healing through loss and renewal. This universal pattern is the way that life perpetuates itself in ever-new forms—ironically, through various kinds of death. This pattern disappoints and scares most of us, but less so biologists and physicists; they seem to understand the pattern better than many clergy, who think death and resurrection is just a doctrinal statement about Jesus.

I am afraid many of us have failed to honor God's always unfolding future and the process of getting there, which usually includes some form of dying to the old. In practical effect, we end up resisting and opposing the very thing we want. The great irony is that we have often done this in the name of praying to God, as though God would protect us from the very process that refines us!

God *protects us into* and *through* death, just as the Father did with Jesus. When this is not made clear, Christianity ends up protecting and idealizing the status quo—or even more, the supposedly wonderful past—at least insofar as it preserves our privilege.

Comfortable people tend to see the church as a quaint antique shop where they can worship old things as substitutes for eternal things.

There is no such thing as a nonpolitical Christianity. To refuse to critique the system or the status quo is to fully support it—which is a political act well disguised. Like Pilate, many Christians choose to wash their hands in front of the crowd and declare themselves innocent, saying with him, "It is your concern" (Matthew 27:25). Pilate maintains his purity and Jesus pays the price. *Going somewhere good means having to go through and with the bad, and being unable to hold ourselves above it or apart from it.* There is no pedestal of perfect purity to stand on, and striving for it is an ego game anyway. Yet the Pilate syndrome is quite common among bona fide Christians, often taking the form of excluding those they consider sinners.

Jesus himself strongly rejects this love of the past and one's private perfection, and he cleverly quotes Isaiah (29:13) to do it: "In vain do they worship me, teaching human precepts as if they were doctrines" (Matthew 15:9). Many of us seem to think that God really is "back there," in the good ol' days of old-time religion when God was really God, and everybody was happy and pure. Such is the illusion of many people attracted to religion, and it is quite popular at many "megachurches" today. All change is private and interior, and any outer critique of systems, one's privilege, one's nation, or one's religion is out of the question. When Jesus first announced "change your mind," he immediately challenged his apostles to leave both their jobs and their families (see Mark 1:20, Matthew 4:22). The change of mind had immediate and major social implications, leading young Jewish men to call two solidly conservative sacred cows—occupation and family—into full question. He did not tell them to attend the synagogue more often or to believe that he was God. Have you ever noted that Jesus never once speaks glowingly of the nuclear family, careers, or jobs? Check it out.

How God Keeps Creation Both Good and New

So, as we bring Part I of this book to a close, let's talk about how God keeps creation both good and new—which means always going somewhere even better. I know some Christians might be hesitant about this, but the helpful word here is "evolution." God keeps creating things from the inside out, so they are forever yearning, developing, growing, and changing for the good. This is the fire he has cast upon the earth, the generative force implanted in all living things, which grows things both from within—because they are programmed for it—and from without—by taking in sun, food, and water.

If we see the Eternal Christ Mystery as the symbolic Alpha Point for the beginning of what we call "time," we can see that history and evolution indeed have an intelligence, a plan, and a trajectory from the very start. The Risen Christ, who appears in the middle of history, assures us that God is leading us somewhere good and positive, all crucifixions to the contrary. God has been leading us since the beginning of time, but now God includes us in the process of unfolding (Romans 8:28–30). This is the opportunity offered us as humans, and those who ride this Christ train are meant to be the "New Humanity" (Ephesians 2:15b). Christ is both the Divine Radiance at the Beginning Big Bang and the Divine Allure drawing us into a positive future. We are thus bookended in a Personal Love—coming *from* Love, and moving *toward* an ever more inclusive Love. This is the Christ Omega! (Rev. 1:6)

Maybe you personally do not feel a need for creation to have any form, direction, or final purpose. After all, many scientists do not seem to ask such ultimate questions. Evolutionists observe the evidence and the data, and say the universe is clearly unfolding and expanding, although they do not know the final goal. But Christians believe the final goal does have a shape and meaning—which is revealed from the way creation began in "very goodness!" Everything that rises does seem to converge. The biblical symbol of the Universal and Eternal Christ standing at both ends of cosmic time was intended to assure us that the clear and full trajectory of the world we know is an unfolding of consciousness with "all creation groaning in this one great act of giving birth" (Romans 8:22).

The New Testament has a clear sense of history working in a way that is both evolutionary and positive. See, for example, Jesus's many parables of the Kingdom, which lean heavily on the language of growth and development. His common metaphors for growth are the seed, the growing ear of corn, weeds and wheat growing together, and the rising of yeast. His parables of the "Reign of God" are almost always about finding, discovering, being surprised, experiencing reversals of expectations, changing roles and status. None of these notions are static; they are always about something new and good coming into being.

Why do I think this is so important? Frankly, because without it we become very impatient with ourselves and others, particularly in the setbacks. Humans and history both grow slowly. We expect people to show up at our doors fully transformed and holy before they can be welcomed in. But growth language says it is appropriate to wait, trusting that *metanoeite*, or change of consciousness, can only come with time—and this patience ends up being the very shape of love. Without it, church becomes the mere enforcing of laws and requirements. "Pastors," instead of serving as caretakers of God's lambs and sheep, are told they should be guards, word police, and dealers in holy antiques. *Without an evolutionary worldview, Christianity does not really understand, much less foster, growth or change. Nor does it know how to respect and support where history is heading.*

The Story Line of Grace

I am looking at a sign here in my office right now that says, LIFE DOES NOT HAVE TO BE PERFECT TO BE WONDERFUL. The steps toward *maturity*, it seems, are always and necessarily *immature*. What else could they be? Good moms and dads learned that a long time ago, and Cardinal John Henry Newman brilliantly captured it when he wrote that "to live is to change, and to be perfect is to have changed often."*

Anything called "Good News" needs to reveal a universal pattern that can be relied upon, and not just clannish or tribal patterns that might be true on occasion. This is probably why Christianity's break with ethnic Judaism was inevitable, although never intended by either Jesus or Paul, and why by the early second century Christians were already calling themselves "catholics" or "the universals." At the front of their consciousness was a belief that God is leading all of history somewhere larger and broader and better for all of humanity. Yet, after Jesus and Paul—except for occasional theologians like Gregory of Nyssa, Athanasius, Maximus the Confessor, and Francis of Assisi—the most widely accepted version of Christianity had little to do with the cosmos or creation, nature or even history. Our beliefs did not generally talk about the future, except in terms of judgment and apocalypse. This is no way to guide history forward; no way to give humanity hope, purpose, direction, or joy.

That is the limited and precarious position Christianity puts itself in when it allows itself to be too tied to any culture-bound Jesus, any expression of faith that does not include the Eternal Christ. Without a universal story line that offers grace and caring

---

* John Henry Newman, *An Essay on the Development of Christian Doctrine* (London: James Toovey, 1845), 39.

for all of creation, Jesus is kept small, and seemingly inept. God's care must be toward all creatures, or God ends up not being very caring at all, making things like water, trees, animals, and history itself accidental, trivial, or disposable. But grace is not a late arrival, an occasional add-on for a handful of humans, and God's grace and life did not just appear a few thousand years ago, when Jesus came and a few lucky humans found him in the Bible. God's grace cannot be a random problem solver doled out to the few and the virtuous— or it is hardly grace at all! (See Ephesians 2:7–10 if you want the radical meaning of grace summed up in three succinct verses.)

What if we recovered this sense of God's inherent grace as the primary generator of all life? And that it does its job from the inside out!

Traces of Goodness

A few years ago, the host of a Scandinavian talk show asked Richard Dawkins, the English biologist and militant atheist, "What is the most common misconception about evolution?" Dawkins's response was "That it is a theory of random chance. It obviously can't be a theory of random chance. If it was a theory of random chance, it couldn't possibly explain why all animals and plants are so beautifully . . . well designed." Dawkins noted that even Darwin himself didn't believe in random chance. "What Darwin did was to discover the only known alternative to random chance, which [he thought] was natural selection."[*]

Yes, he actually said that! Dawkins is leaving the door fully open for what some call "intelligent design," but let's not fight about the

---

[*] Richard Dawkins, "Richard Dawkins on *Skavlan*," *Skavlan*, YouTube, December 2015, https://www.youtube.com/watch?v=e3oae0AOQew.

wording. As a result of this fight, many educated people no longer want to talk with religious people, or use our phraseology. Thus the dead-ended culture wars we are involved in today where each side is entrenched behind symbolic words.

All I know is that creationists and evolutionists do not have to be enemies. The evolutionists rightly want to say the universe is unfolding, while believers can rightly insist on the personal meaning of that unfolding. We give the phenomenon of life and matter a positive and certain end point, which we call "resurrection," while also accounting for lots of suffering and death along the way, which we call "crucifixion." That is, indeed, a momentous and grand vision, and it explains a lot, but it also carries so much extra baggage that I can see why rational and scientifically minded folks usually resist it.

Yet to believe that Jesus was raised from the dead is actually not a leap of faith. *Resurrection and renewal are, in fact, the universal and observable pattern of everything.* We might just as well use nonreligious terms like "springtime," "regeneration," "healing," "forgiveness," "life cycles," "darkness," and "light." If incarnation is real, then resurrection in multitudinous forms is to be fully expected. Or to paraphrase that earlier statement attributed to Albert Einstein, it is not that one thing is a miracle, but that the whole thing is a miracle!

This point is worth sitting with for a few moments.

Every time you take in a breath, you are repeating the pattern of taking spirit into matter, and thus repeating the first creation of Adam.

And every time you breathe out, you are repeating the pattern of returning spirit to the material universe. In a way, every exhalation is a "little dying" as we pay the price of inspiriting the world.

Your simple breathing models your entire vocation as a human being. You are an incarnation, like Christ, of matter and spirit operating as one. This, more than anything we believe or accomplish, is how all of us continue the mystery of incarnation in space and time—either knowingly and joyfully—or not.

If divine incarnation has any truth to it, then resurrection is a foregone conclusion, and not a one-time anomaly in the body of Jesus, as our Western understanding of the resurrection felt it needed to prove—and then it couldn't. *The Risen Christ is not a one-time miracle but the revelation of a universal pattern that is hard to see in the short run.*

The job for believers is to figure out not the *how* or the *when* of resurrection, but just the *what!* Leave the how and the when to science and to God. True Christianity and true science are both transformational worldviews that place growth and development at their centers. Both endeavors, each in its own way, cooperate with some Divine Plan, and whether God is formally acknowledged may not be that important. As C. G. Jung inscribed over his doorway, *Vocatus atque non vocatus, Deus aderit,* "Invoked or not invoked, God is still present."*

God has worked anonymously since the very beginning—it has always been an inside and secret sort of job.

The Spirit seems to work best underground. When aboveground, humans start fighting about it.

You can call this grace, the indwelling Holy Spirit, or just evolution toward union (which we call "love"). God is not in competition with anybody, but *only in deep-time cooperation with everybody who loves* (Romans 8:28). Whenever we place one caring foot forward, God uses it, sustains it, and blesses it. Our impulse does not need to wear the name of religion at all.

Love is the energy that sustains the universe, moving us toward a future of resurrection. We do not even need to call it love or God or resurrection for its work to be done.

---

* G. G. Jung, *Letters: 1951–1961,* vol. 2, ed. G. Adler (Princeton, NJ: Princeton University Press, 1975), 611.

PART 2

THE GREAT COMMA

8

Doing and Saying

. . . Born of the Virgin Mary,
suffered under Pontius Pilate . . .
—The Apostles' Creed

If you worship in one of the more liturgical Christian traditions, you probably know the opening words of the Apostles' Creed by heart:

> I believe in God, the Father Almighty, creator of heaven and earth. I believe in Jesus Christ, his only Son, our Lord, who was conceived by the Holy Spirit, born of the Virgin Mary, suffered under Pontius Pilate, was crucified, died, and was buried; he descended into hell . . .

But have you ever noticed the huge leap the creed makes between "born of the Virgin Mary" and "suffered under Pontius Pilate"? *A single comma* connects the two statements, and falling into that yawning gap, as if it were a mere detail, is *everything* Jesus said and did between his birth and his death! Called the "Great Comma," this gap certainly invites some serious questions. Did all the things Jesus said and did in those years not count for much? Were they nothing to "believe" in? Was it only his birth and death that mattered? Does the gap in some way explain Christianity's often dismal record of imitating Jesus's actual life and teaching?

There are other glaring oversights in the creeds. Believed to be the earliest formal declaration of Christian belief, the Apostles' Creed does not once mention love, service, hope, the "least of the brothers and sisters," or even forgiveness—anything, actually, that is remotely *actionable*. It's a vision and philosophy statement with no mission statement, as it were. Twice we are reminded that God is almighty, yet nowhere do we hear mention that God is also *all suffering* or *all vulnerable* (although it does declare that Jesus "suffered . . . , died, and was buried"). With its emphasis on theory and theology, but no emphasis on praxis—the creed set us on a course we are still following today.

The Apostles' Creed, along with the later Nicene Creed, is an important document of theological summary and history, but when the crowd at my parish mumbles hurriedly through its recitation each Sunday, I'm struck by how little usefulness—or even interest—the creeds seem to bring as guides for people's daily, practical behavior. I hope I am wrong, but I doubt it.

Both creeds reveal historic Christian assumptions about who God is and what God is doing. They reaffirm a static and unchanging universe, and a God who is quite remote from almost everything we care about each day. Furthermore, they don't show much interest in the realities of Jesus's own human life—or ours. Instead, they portray what religious systems tend to want: a God who looks strong and stable and in control. No "turn the other cheek" Jesus, no hint of a simple Christ-like lifestyle is found here.

You might wonder why I'm bothering you with this bit of historical and theological trivia. Here is the reason:

When our tradition chose an imperial Christ who lives inside the world of static and mythic proclamations, it framed Christian belief and understanding in a very small box. The Christ of these creeds is not tethered to earth—to a real, historical, flesh-and-blood Jesus of Nazareth. Instead, it is mostly mind with little heart, all spirit and almost no flesh or soul. Is our only mission to merely keep announcing our vision and philosophy statement? Sometimes it has seemed that way. This is what happens when power and empire take over the message.

Did you know that the first seven Councils of the Church, agreed upon by both East and West, were all either convened or formally presided over by emperors? This is no small point. Emperors and governments do not tend to be interested in an ethic of love, or service, or nonviolence (God forbid!), and surely not forgiveness unless it somehow helps them stay in power.

For all who have tried to know Jesus without Christ, many of the core church teachings offered a disembodied Christ without any truly human Jesus, which was the norm for centuries in doctrine and in art. *Art is the giveaway of what people really believe at any one time.* It bears repeating what John Dominic Crossan demonstrated in his masterful study about Eastern and Western images of the Resurrection; we had two extremely different theologies of its very meaning. The West declared, "Jesus rose from the dead" as an individual; the Eastern church saw it in at least three ways: *the trampling of hell, the corporate leading out of hell, and the corporate uplifting of humanity with Christ.* That is a quite different message. But after 1054 we had little knowledge of each other, since

---

* Crossan, *Resurrecting Easter,* especially 153ff.

each considered the other side heretical. Perhaps this was the worst historical result of our dualistic (noncontemplative) thinking and practice. All that remained in the Western church was the one line in that same Apostles' Creed, "He descended into hell," but no one really was sure what that meant.

In the second half of this book, I'd like to consider how an understanding of the Christ can revolutionize how we practice our faith, in ways big and small. For me, mere information is rarely helpful unless it also enlightens and "amorizes" your life. In Franciscan theology, *truth is always for the sake of love—and not an absolute end in itself, which too often becomes the worship of an ideology.* In other words, any good idea that does not engage the body, the heart, the physical world, and the people around us will tend to be more theological problem solving and theory than any real healing of people and institutions—which ironically is about all Jesus does! The word "healing" did not return to mainline Christian vocabulary until the 1970s,* and even then it was widely resisted, which I know from my own experience. In the Catholic tradition, we had pushed healing off till the very last hour of life and called the Sacrament "Extreme Unction," apparently not aware that Jesus provided free health care in the middle of life for people who were suffering, and it was not just an "extreme" measure to get them into the next world.

You wouldn't guess this from the official creeds, but after all is said and done, doing is more important than saying. Jesus was clearly more concerned with what Buddhists call "right action" ("orthopraxy" in Christianity) than with right saying, or even right

---

* Francis McNutt, *Healing* (Notre Dame, IN: Ave Maria Press, 1974). I worked with Francis in the 1970s and witnessed many levels of healing with my own eyes. Just as in the Gospels, it caused much fear, pushback, and denial from the "faithful."

thinking. You can hear this message very clearly in his parable of the two sons in Matthew 21:28–31: One son says he won't work in the vineyard, but then does, while the other says he will go, but in fact doesn't. Jesus told his listeners that he preferred the one who actually goes although saying the wrong words, over the one who says the right words but does not act. How did we miss that?

Humanity now needs a Jesus who is historical, relevant for real life, physical and concrete, like we are. A Jesus whose life can save you even more than his death. A Jesus we can practically imitate, and who sets the bar for what it means to be fully human. And a Christ who is big enough to hold all creation together in one harmonious unity.

In the remaining pages of this book, allow me to offer you such a Jesus and such a Christ.

9

Things at Their Depth

One day the religion of Christ will take another step forward on earth. It will embrace the whole man [sic], all of him, not just half as it does now in embracing only the soul.

—Nikos Kazantzakis, *Report to Greco*

As I watch Catholics receive communion at Mass, I notice that some, after taking the bread and wine, turn toward the altar or the sacred box that reserves the bread and bow or genuflect as a gesture of respect—as if the Presence were still over there. In those moments, I wonder if they have missed what just happened! Don't they realize that the Eucharist was supposed to be a full transference of identity *to them*? They themselves are now the living, moving tabernacle, just like the Ark of the Covenant. Is this too much for them to imagine? Does it seem presumptuous and impossible? It appears so.

Likewise, I have known many Evangelicals who "received Jesus into their hearts" but still felt the need to "get saved" again every Friday night. Did they not believe that a real transformation happened if they made a genuine surrender and reconnected to their Source? Most of us understandably start the journey assuming that God is "up there," and our job is to transcend this world to find "him." We spend so much time trying to get "up there," we miss that God's big leap in Jesus was to come "down here." So much of our worship and religious effort is the spiritual equivalent of trying to go up what has become the down escalator.

I suspect that the "up there" mentality is the way most people's spiritual search has to start. But once the real inner journey begins—once you come to know that in Christ, God is forever overcoming the gap between human and divine—the Christian path becomes less about climbing and performance, and more about descending, letting go, and unlearning. Knowing and loving Jesus is largely about becoming fully human, wounds and all, instead of ascending spiritually or thinking we can remain unwounded. (The ego does not like this fundamental switch at all, so we keep returning to some kind of performance principle, trying to climb out of this messy incarnation instead of learning from it. This is most early-stage religion.)

Jesus offered the world a living example of fully embodied Love that emerged out of our ordinary, limited life situations. For me, this is the real import of Paul's statement that Jesus was "born of a woman under the Law" (Galatians 4:4). In Jesus, God became part of our small, homely world and entered into human limits and ordinariness—and remained anonymous and largely invisible for his first thirty years. Throughout his life, Jesus himself spent no time climbing, but a lot of time descending, *"emptying himself and becoming as all humans are"* (Philippians 2:7), "tempted in every way that we are" (Hebrews 4:15) and "living in the limitations of weakness" (Hebrews 5:2). In this chapter, I would like to consider such a path, and what it means for you and me.

The Divine Map

Jesus walked, enjoyed, and suffered the entire human journey, and he told us that we could and should do the same. His life exemplified the unfolding mystery in all of its stages—from a hidden, divine conception, to a regular adult life full of love and problems, punctuated by a few moments of transfiguration and enlightenment, and all leading to glorious ascension and final return. As Hebrews 4:15 says, "For we do not have a high priest who is unable to sympathize with our weakness, but we have one who was like us in every way, experienced every temptation, and never backtracked" (my translation). We do not need to be afraid of the depths and breadths of our own lives, of what this world offers us or asks of us. We are given permission to become intimate with our own experiences, learn from them, and allow ourselves to descend to the depth of things, even our mistakes, before we try too quickly to transcend it all in the name of some idealized purity or superiority. *God hides in the depths and is not seen as long as we stay on the surface of anything— even the depths of our sins.*

Remember, the archetypal encounter between doubting Thomas and the Risen Jesus (John 20:19–28) is not really a story about believing in the fact of the resurrection, but a story about believing that someone could *be wounded and also resurrected at the same time!* That is a quite different message, and still desperately needed. "Put your finger here," Jesus says to Thomas (20:27). And, like Thomas, we are indeed wounded and resurrected at the same time, all of us. In fact, this might be the primary pastoral message of the whole Gospel.

Earlier, I wrote that great love and great suffering (both healing and woundedness) are the universal, always available paths of transformation, because they are the only things strong enough to take away the ego's protections and pretensions. Great love and great suffering bring us back to God, with the second normally following the first, and I believe this is how Jesus himself walked humanity back to God. It is not just a path of resurrection rewards, but always a path that includes death and woundedness.

St. Bonaventure (1221–1274) taught that, "As a human being Christ has something in common with all creatures. With the stones he shares existence, with plants he shares life, with animals he shares sensation, and with the angels he shares intelligence."* In saying this, Bonaventure was trying to give theological weight to the deep experience of St. Francis of Assisi (1181–1226), who as far as we know, was the first recorded Christian to call animals and elements and even the forces of nature by familial names: "Sister, Mother Earth," "Brother Wind," "Sister Water," and "Brother Fire."

Francis was fully at home in this created world. He saw all things in the visible world as endless dynamic and operative symbols of the Real, a theater and training ground for a heaven that is already available to us in small doses in this life. *What you choose now, you shall have later* seems to be the realization of the saints. Not an idyllic hope for a later heaven but a living experience right now.

We cannot jump over this world, or its woundedness, and still try to love God. We must love God *through, in, with,* and even *because of* this world. This is the message Christianity was supposed to initiate, proclaim, and encourage, and what Jesus modeled. We

---

* Bonaventure, *Sermon I, Dom II in Quad.* (IX, 215–219), trans. Zachary Hayes, "Christ Word of God and Exemplar of Humanity," *The Lord* 46.1 (1996): 13.

were made to love and trust this world, "to cultivate it and take care of it" (Genesis 2:15), but for some sad reason we preferred to emphasize the statement that comes three verses later, which seems to say that we should "dominate" the earth (1:28), where within one generation we become killers of our brothers (Genesis 4:8). I wonder if this is not another shape of our original sin. God "empties himself" into creation (Philippians 2:7), and then we humans spent most of history creating systems to control and subdue that creation for our own purposes and profit, reversing the divine pattern.

Do not think I am talking about believing only what you can see with your eyes, or proposing mere materialism. I am talking about *observing, touching, loving the physical, the material, the inspirited universe—in all of its suffering state—*as the necessary starting place for any healthy spirituality and any true development. Death *and* resurrection, not death *or* resurrection. This is indeed the depth of everything. *To stay on the surface of anything is invariably to miss its message—even the surface meaning of our sinfulness.*

Jesus invited Thomas and all doubters into a *tangible* kind of religion, a religion that makes touching human pain and suffering the way into both compassion and understanding. For most of us, the mere touching of another's wound probably feels like an act of outward kindness; we don't realize that its full intended effect is to change us as much as it might change them (there is no indication that Jesus changed, only Thomas). Human sympathy is the best and easiest way to open the heart space and to make us live inside our own bodies. God never intended most human beings to become philosophers or theologians, but God does want all humans to represent the very Sympathy and Empathy of God. And it's okay if it takes a while to get there.

Our central message again bears repeating: *God loves things by becoming them. We love God by continuing the same pattern.*

Always and Only the Incarnation

Christianity's unique trump card is always and forever incarnation. This is why the only heresies that have been condemned in every century under different names are those that sought to deny the Incarnation, or undermine it with heady spiritualism or pious romanticism. This tendency was generically called "Gnosticism," and I sometimes wonder if the church condemned it so much because we unconsciously knew how heady and Gnostic we ourselves were. "Condemn it over there instead of own it over here" is the operative and common policy of institutions of power. But as the poet and wisdom figure Wendell Berry loves to tell us, *"What we need is here."** Humanity has grown tired of grand, overarching societal plans like communism and Nazism, and of disembodied spiritualities that allow no validation or verification in experience. Too often they hide an agenda of power and control, obfuscating and distracting us from what is right in front of us. This is exactly what we do when we make the emphasis of Jesus's Gospel what is "out there" as opposed to what is "in here." For example, insisting on a literal belief in the virgin birth of Jesus is very good theological symbolism, but unless it translates into a spirituality of interior poverty, readiness to conceive, and human vulnerability, it is largely a "mere lesson memorized" as Isaiah puts it (29:13). It "saves" no one. Likewise, an intellectual belief that Jesus rose from the dead is a good start, but until you are struck by the realization that the crucified and risen Jesus is a parable about the journey of all humans, and even the universe, it is a rather harmless—if not harmful—belief that will leave you and the world largely unchanged.

We are now acquiring and accessing more of the skills we need

---

* Wendell Berry, "The Wild Geese," in *Collected Poems* (Berkeley: North Point Press, 1984), 155–156.

to go into the depths of things—and to find God's spirit there. Whether they come through psychology, trained spiritual direction, the Enneagram, Myers-Briggs typology, grief and bereavement work, or other models such as Integral Theory or wilderness training,* these tools help us to examine and to trust interiority and depth as never before. One of the most profound spiritual experiences of my life came in 1984, during a journaling retreat led by the psychotherapist Ira Progoff. At this retreat, held in Dayton, Ohio, Progoff guided us as we wrote privately for several days on some very human but ordinary questions. I remember first dialoguing with my own body, dialoguing with roads not taken, dialoguing with concrete events and persons, dialoguing with my own past decisions, on and on.

I learned that if the quiet space, the questions themselves, and blank pages had not been put in front of me, I may never have known what was lying within me. Dr. Progoff helped me and many others access slow tears and fast prayers, and ultimately often intense happiness and gratitude, as I discovered depths within myself that I never knew were there. I still reread some of what I wrote over forty years ago for encouragement and healing. And it all came from within me!

Today we have freedom and permission and the tools to move toward depth as few people ever had in human history. What a shame it would be if we did not use them. The best way *out* is if we have first gone *in*. The only way we can trust *up* is if we have gone *down*. That had been the underlying assumption of male initiation rites since ancient times, but today, such inner journeys, basic initiation experiences, are often considered peripheral to "true religion."

---

* Illuman.org, Outward Bound, Bill Plotkin Animas training, New Warrior Training, et cetera.

Permission to Go "In" and "Down"

If you think I am emphasizing the experiential too much, just remember that both Jesus and Paul trusted their own experience of
God against the status quo of their own Jewish religion. This deep
trust led Paul to oppose Peter, the supposed first Pope, "to his face"
over the issue of whether Gentile converts should be required to un-
dergo the Jewish rite of circumcision (Galatians 2:11–13). Paul and
his ministry partner, Barnabas, soon repeated the same arguments
to the whole leadership team of early Christianity in Jerusalem
(Acts 15:1–12), and further insisted on the inclusion of the entire
Gentile world (which is most of us). And they did so with no justification of authority beyond whatever it was that Paul *experienced*
on the Damascus Road and thereafter. Paul rejecting circumcision,
as he does more than once (see Galatians 5:12), would be like me
denying the importance of baptism. Jesus defending his disciples'
practice of working on the Sabbath (Matthew 12:1ff.) would be like
me saying that Mass on Tuesday is just as good as Mass on Sunday. (Of course, it actually is, except for the historic consensus that
Sunday is the agreed-upon time for community worship.) "By what
authority are you doing these things? And who gave you this authority?" the priests and elders rightly ask (Matthew 21:23) of Jesus. I
must admit that I would probably have asked the same hard questions of both Jesus and Paul.

It's no stretch to say that the New Testament faith was, in effect,
written by two men who profoundly relied upon their inner experience of the ways of God despite a totally dominant consciousness
that insisted otherwise. How did they get away with it? The answer is, in their lifetimes, they largely didn't. Only later did saints
and scholars see that Jesus and Paul had drawn upon the deepest
sources of their own tradition to then totally reframe that tradition
for the larger world. They, like all the prophets, were "radical tradi-

tionalists." *You can only reform things long term by unlocking them from inside—by their own chosen authoritative sources.* Outsiders have little authority or ability to reform anything.

All traditions and traditionalists are searching for sacred objects, places, events, and people on which to found their authority, and this is normal and good. Once we find such a foundation, we make pilgrimages, write scriptures, visit tombs, create customs till they become sacrosanct traditions. We kiss holy rocks, paint art, create sacred architecture, weep with sincerity, and offer devotion to our symbol of the Absolute. But these totems, rituals, tombs (or empty tomb, in our case), and holy places are just early signposts to set us on the path. The full mystery of incarnation, on the other hand, points not just to things, but to the *depth* of things, the fullness of things, the soul of things, and what some have called the "angels of things."

In his book *Unmasking the Powers* theologian and biblical scholar Walter Wink makes a very convincing case that this intuition about the inherent sacredness of creation is precisely what sacred texts are pointing toward when they speak of "angels."* An angel, Wink believed, is *the inner spirit or soul of a thing.* When we honor the "angel" or soul of a thing, we respect its inner spirit. And if we learn how to pay attention to the soul of things—to see the "angels" of elements, animals, the earth, water, and skies—then we can naturally work our way back through the Great Chain of Being to the final link, whom many call God. Don't waste your time deconstructing your primitive belief about pretty, winged creatures in flowing pastel dresses. If you do so, you are seriously missing out on what they are pointing to. *We need to reconstruct, and not just continue to deconstruct.* Then you will see angels everywhere.

---

* Walter Wink, *Unmasking the Powers: The Invisible Forces That Determine Human Existence* (Philadelphia: Fortress Press, 1986).

What I am saying in this chapter is that there must be a way to be both *here* and in the *depth of here*. Jesus is the here, Christ is the depth of here. This, in my mind, is the essence of incarnation, and the gift of contemplation. We must learn to love and enjoy things as they are, in their depth, in their soul, and in their fullness. Contemplation is the "second gaze," through which you see something in its particularity and yet also in a much larger frame. You know it by the joy it gives, which is far greater than anything it does for you in terms of money, power, or success.

Two pieces of art have given me this incarnational and contemplative insight. The first was one I saw in a Nuremberg art museum by Hans Kulmbach. It portrays the two human feet of Jesus at the very top of a large painting of the Ascension. Most of the canvas is taken up by the apostles, who are being drawn up with Christ with their eyes, as the two feet move off the top of the painting, presumably into the spiritual realms. The image had a wonderful effect on me. I too found myself looking beyond the painting toward the ceiling of the art museum, my eyes drawn elsewhere for the message. It was a real religious moment, one that simultaneously took me beyond the painting and right back into the room where I was standing. It was another instance of understanding the Christ in a collective sense, not just his ascension but also ours. Look at texts like Colossians 2:11–15 and Ephesians 2:4–6, and notice how they clearly present salvation in both the past tense and the collective sense. Why did we never notice this?

The second piece of art is a bronze statue of St. Francis, located in the upper basilica of Assisi, Italy. Created by a sculptor whose name is hidden, the statue shows Francis gazing down into the dirt with awe and wonder, which is quite unusual and almost shocking. The Holy Spirit, who is almost always pictured as descending from above, is pictured here as coming from below—even to the point of being hidden in the dirt! I've made sure I go see this statue whenever I return to Assisi, but I fear most people miss it, because it is small and set off to the side—just like the Christ message itself. "Truly, you are a hidden God," Isaiah says (45:15). God is hidden in the dirt and mud instead of descending from the clouds. This is a major transposition of place. Once you know that the miracle of "Word made flesh" has become the very nature of the universe, you cannot help but be both happy and holy. What we first of all need is here!

Both these pieces of art put the two worlds together, just from different perspectives. Yet in both images, *it is the Divine that takes the lead in changing places.* Maybe artists have easier access to this Mystery than many theologians? The right brain often gets there faster and more easily than the left brain, and we let the left brainers take over our churches.

I doubt if you can see the image of God (*Imago Dei*) in your fellow humans if you cannot first see it in rudimentary form in stones, in plants and flowers, in strange little animals, in bread and wine, and most especially cannot honor this objective divine image in yourself. It is a full-body tune-up, this spiritual journey. It really ends up being *all or nothing, here and then everywhere.*

Respect, Wonder, Reverence

This change of perspective, to bottom up and inside out, can take the form of religious language or totally secular language. Words are not the reality itself (the *Ding an sich,* as the Germans say). We all know *respect* when we see it (re-spect = to see a second time). We all know reverence because it softens our gaze. *Any object that calls forth respect or reverence is the "Christ" or the anointed one for us at that moment,* even though the conduit might just look like a committed research scientist, an old man cleaning up the beach, a woman going the extra mile for her neighbor, an earnest, eager dog licking your face, or an ascent of pigeons across the plaza.

All people who see with that second kind of contemplative gaze, all who look at the world with respect, even if they are not formally religious, are *en Cristo,* or in Christ. For them, as Thomas Merton says, "the gate of heaven is everywhere" because of their freedom to respect what is right in front of them—all the time.*

---

* Thomas Merton, *Conjectures of a Guilty Bystander* (Garden City, NY: Doubleday, 1966), 142.

10

The Feminine Incarnation

From now on, all generations will call me blessed;
for the Mighty One has done great things for me, and
holy is his name.

—Luke 1:48–49

I am going to take some risks in this brief chapter, but I believe it will be worthwhile because for many, this could invite the most important breakthrough of all. Since I am a man, my own perspective on the feminine is surely limited, but this is such a crucial and often ignored theme that I must invite us all to reclaim and honor female wisdom, which is often *qualitatively* different from male wisdom. I will draw from my own experiences with my mother (I was her favorite), sisters before and behind me, many women friends and colleagues over the years, and the very nature of some of my God encounters. I hope this perspective can invite you to trust your own experiences with the divine feminine as well. For many, it is an utterly new opening, since they always falsely assumed that God is somehow masculine.

Although Jesus was clearly of the masculine gender, the Christ is beyond gender, and so it should be expected that the Big Tradition would have found feminine ways, consciously or unconsciously, to symbolize the full Divine Incarnation and to give God a more feminine character—as the Bible itself often does.*

Whenever I go to Europe, I am always struck by how many churches bear the name of Mary, Jesus's mother. I think I encountered a "Notre Dame of something" church in every French city I ever visited, and sometimes even two or three in one small town. Some of these churches are big and ornate, most are very old, and they usually inspire respect and devotion, even among nonbelievers. Yet even as a Catholic I sometimes wonder, Who were these Christian people who appear to have honored Mary much more than Jesus? After all, the New Testament speaks very little of Mary. No wonder the Protestant Reformation reacted so strongly against our Orthodox and Catholic preoccupation!

Why did the first fourteen hundred years of Christianity, in both the Eastern and Western churches, fall head over heels in love with this seemingly quite ordinary woman? We gave her names like *Theotokos*, Mother of God, Queen of Heaven, *Notre Dame, La Virgen* of this or that, *Unsere Liebe Frau, Nuestra Señora,* Our Mother of Sorrows, Our Lady of Perpetual Help, and Our Lady of just about

---

* After the sixteenth century, when Westerners became more rational and literate, most of us stopped thinking symbolically, allegorically, or typologically. But in so doing, we lost something quite important in our spiritual, intuitive, and nonrational understanding of God and ourselves. We narrowed the field considerably and actually lessened the likelihood of inner religious experience. The Bible became an excuse for *not* learning how literature "works." Catholics were on symbolic overload; Protestants reacted and became symbolically starved.

every village or shrine in Europe. We are clearly dealing with not just a single woman here but a foundational symbol—or, to borrow the language of Carl Jung, an "archetype"—an image that constellates a whole host of meanings that cannot be communicated logically. Nothing emerges that broadly and over so much of time if it is not grounded somehow in our collective human unconscious. One would be foolish to dismiss such things lightly.

In the mythic imagination, I think Mary intuitively symbolizes the first Incarnation—or Mother Earth, if you will allow me. (I am not saying Mary *is* the first incarnation, only that she became the natural archetype and symbol for it, particularly in art, which is perhaps why the Madonna is still the most painted subject in Western art.) I believe that Mary is the major feminine archetype for the Christ Mystery. This archetype had already shown herself as *Sophia* or Holy Wisdom (see Proverbs 8:1ff., Wisdom 7:7ff.), and again in the book of Revelation (12:1–17) in the cosmic symbol of "a Woman clothed with the sun and standing on the moon." Neither Sophia nor the Woman of Revelation is precisely Mary of Nazareth, yet in so many ways, both are—and each broadens our understanding of the Divine Feminine.

Jung believed that humans produce in art *the inner images the soul needs in order to see itself and to allow its own transformation.* Just try to count how many paintings in world art museums, churches, and homes show a wonderfully dressed woman offering for your admiration—and hers—a usually naked baby boy. What is the very ubiquity of this image saying on the soul level? I think it looks something like this:

The first incarnation (creation) is symbolized by Sophia-Incarnate, a beautiful, feminine, multicolored, graceful Mary.

She is invariably offering us Jesus, God incarnated into vulnerability and nakedness.

Mary became the Symbol of the First Universal Incarnation.

She then hands the Second Incarnation on to us, while remaining in the background; the focus is always on the child.

Earth Mother presenting Spiritual Son, the two first stages of the Incarnation.

Feminine Receptivity, handing on the fruit of her yes.

And inviting us to offer our own yes.

There is a wholeness about this that many find very satisfying to the soul.

I hope you will not write this line of thinking off as trendy feminism, or simply an attempt to address the concerns of those who have left Christianity because of the sins of patriarchy, or the church's failure to recognize and honor a feminine understanding of God. We always had the feminine incarnation, in fact it was the first incarnation, and even better, it moved toward including all of us! *Mary is all of us* both *receiving and handing on the gift.* We liked her precisely because she was one of us—and *not* God!

I think Christians of the first thousand years understood this on an intuitive and allegorical level. But by the time of the much-needed Protestant Reformation, all we could see was "but she is not God." Which is entirely true. But we could no longer see in wholes, and see that even better, "She is us!" That is why we loved her, probably without fully understanding why. (Much of the human race can more easily imagine unconditional love coming from the feminine and the maternal more than from a man.) I have to say this!

In the many images of Mary, humans see our own feminine soul. We needed to see ourselves in her, and say with her "God has looked upon me in my lowliness. From now on, all generations will call me blessed" (Luke 1:48).

I do realize the dangers here, and I acknowledge that for all practical purposes many Catholics divinized Mary, probably out of sentimentality. All the same, I invite you to consider the deeper and more subtle message. I have often said that many Catholics have a poor theology of Mary but an excellent psychology: *Humans like, need, and trust our mothers to give us gifts, to nurture us, and always to forgive us, which is what we want from God.* My years of work with men's groups have convinced me of it. In fact, the more macho and patriarchal a culture, the greater its devotion to Mary. I once counted eleven images of Mary in a single Catholic church in Texas cowboy country. I see that as a culture trying unconsciously, and often not very successfully, to balance itself out. In the same way, Mary gives women in the Catholic church a dominant feminine image to counterbalance all the males parading around up front!

Humanity has always been receiving the Christ in every culture and age, and women are most naturally imaged as the receivers of the Divine Gift: Think Willendorf, Ephesus, Constantinople, Ravenna, Mt. Carmel, Black Madonnas, Valencia, Walsingham, Guadalupe, until every country of the world eventually had its own feminine image, of one who has received the Christ in her very body (not in her head!). And also note the rather universal pronoun "our," always "*Our* Lady," never "*my* Lady." This is a sure giveaway that we are dealing with a Corporate Personality (one who stands for the whole) and a collective understanding of salvation. Same with "Our Lord" or "Our Father." I never hear official liturgical prayers speak of "my Jesus" or "my Lord." God and Mary are always addressed as a shared experience, at least in the historic churches, and before our later individualization of the whole Gospel message.

I find it interesting that male gods *tend* to come from the heavens, and are usually associated with the sun, sky, power, and light. But in most mythology and fairy tales, feminine gods tend to come out of the earth or the sea and are often associated with fertility, subtlety, good darkness, and nurturance. Invariably "Brother Sun" and "Sister Moon," except in German! If creation is indeed the first Incarnation and the "first Bible" (Romans 1:20), if mother precedes child, then it is not at all surprising that the physical, earthly, and embodied symbols would be recognized in mind, art, and tradition as "Mother Earth" (never "Father"). From this intuition the first fourteen hundred years of Christianity, East and West, made an easy transference to Mary, who was invariably clothed in flowing beauty and color, often crowned by Jesus, and was no longer the simple, poor maiden of Nazareth.

Another important nonbiblical emergence was the widespread belief that Mary's body was taken up into heaven after her death. (This is the only example I know of the Vatican actually taking a survey before it proclaimed the doctrine, in 1950. They found that most of the Catholic world already believed this to be true without it ever having been taught formally, which is called the *sensus fidelium*.) Accounts of Mary's Assumption aren't found anywhere in the Bible—unless you want to read Revelation 12 in that archetypal way—but they circulated among Christians as early as the fourth century. And by the time the Vatican formalized the doctrine, Carl Jung considered the confirmation "the most significant theological development of the twentieth century" because it proclaimed that a *woman's body* permanently exists in the eternal realms! Wow. The pantheon of male god images was forever feminized, and even more, it was declared that human bodies, not just souls or spirits, could share in the process of divinization. This is hugely important. The Mary symbol brought together the two disparate worlds of matter and spirit, feminine mother and masculine child, earth and heaven, whether we like it or not. The unconscious got it, I think. Consciously, many fought it—to their own loss, in my opinion. Now much of the world sees Christianity as hopelessly patriarchal.

Saying Yes to God

The point is that in some ways, many humans can identify with Mary more than they can with Jesus precisely because she was *not* God, but the archetype for our yes to God! Not one heroic action is attributed to her, only trust itself. *Pure being and not doing.* From her first yes to the angel Gabriel (Luke 1:38), to the birth itself (2:7), to her last yes at the foot of the cross (John 19:25), and her full presence at fiery, windy Pentecost (see Acts 1:14, where she is the only woman named at the first outpouring of the Spirit), Mary appears on cue at the key moments of the Gospel narratives. She is Everywoman and Everyman, and that is why I call her the feminine symbol for the universal incarnation.

Mary is the Great Yes that humanity forever needs for Christ to be born into the world. Even Paul McCartney immortalized this idea in his song "Let It Be," although on the first level he was talking about his own mother, Mary:

> *Mother Mary comes to me,*
> *Speaking words of wisdom, "Let it be."*

That's why people in the first thousand years loved her so much. In Mary, we see that God must never be forced on us, and God never comes uninvited.

If Christ and Jesus are the archetypes of what God is doing, Mary is the archetype of *how to receive what God is doing* and *hand it on to others.* In art, she is invariably offering Jesus to the observer or inviting us to come to him. "To Jesus through Mary" we Catholics used to say in the 1950s. Again, very poor theology but very effective psychology and pedagogy for many.

In Mary, humanity has said *our* eternal yes to God.

A yes that cannot be undone.

A corporate yes that overrides our many noes.

This is why Mary was commonly called the "New Eve," who undid the corporate no of the first Eve, and is invariably pictured in art stepping on the snake that tempted Eve (Genesis 3:15).

Today on many levels, we are witnessing an immense longing for the mature feminine at every level of our society—from our politics, to our economics, in our psyche, our cultures, our patterns of leadership, and our theologies, all of which have become far too warlike, competitive, mechanistic, and noncontemplative. We are terribly imbalanced.

Far too often the feminine has had to work in secret, behind the scenes, indirectly. Yet it can still have a profound effect. We see Mary's subtlety of grace, patience, and humility when she quietly says at the wedding feast of Cana, "They have no wine" (John 2:3b), and then seems totally assured that Jesus will take it from there (John 2:5). And he does!

Like the Christ Mystery itself, *the deep feminine* often works underground and in the shadows, and—from that position—creates a much more intoxicating message. While church and culture have often denied the Divine Feminine roles, offices, and formal authority, the feminine has continued to exercise incredible power at the cosmic and personal levels. Most of us in the American Catholic church feel that the culture of faith was passed on to us much more from the nuns than from the priests. Feminine power is deeply relational and symbolic—and thus transformative—in ways that men cannot control or even understand. I suspect that is why we fear it so much.

11

This Is My Body

Life is the destiny you are bound to refuse
until you have consented to die.

—W. H. Auden, "For the Time Being"

In my fifty years as a priest, I would guess I have celebrated the Eucharistic Meal (also known as the Lord's Supper) thousands of times. I cannot say it was the center of my life, although presiding over the liturgy surely gave me many wonderful occasions to serve people in different settings and cultures, and, I hope, to preach an enlivening word in that context. Most often it was a true experience of "communion," as ordinary Catholics usually speak of it—communion with God and with God's people, and often with myself. I knew and accepted the orthodox theology of Eucharist and offered the prayers gladly, although I often changed them when they implied the wrong thing. It was all good, something that I took for granted as part of my work and my faith.

But a few years ago, a new and compelling message made its way into my mind and heart and body. I realized that Jesus did not say, "This is my spirit, given for you," or even "These are my thoughts." Instead, he very daringly said, "This is my *body*," which seems like an overly physical and risky way for a spiritual teacher, a God-man, to speak. Indeed, Jesus's raw proclamation did shock its first hearers. As John reports, "Many left him and stopped going with him" (John 6:66). Incarnation is always somehow a scandal, "too much" for us to deal with!

For most of us, "giving" our body to another person connotes something intimate, deeply personal, and often sexual. Did Jesus know this? Why would he talk this way and bring his spiritual message down to such a "fleshly" level? "My flesh is real food, my blood is real drink," he insisted (John 6:55). Frankly, even today it sounds naïve, off-putting, and even cannibalistic. The very word John uses here, *sarx,* is the same word Paul uses throughout his letters to describe the opposite of spirit. He does not use the softer word for body, *soma.* This is quite amazing to me.

I have come to realize that, in offering his body, *Jesus is precisely giving us his full bodily humanity more than his spiritualized divinity!* "Eat me," he shockingly says, eating being such a fundamental bodily action, more basic and primitive than thinking or talking. The very fleshly humanity that Paul later presents negatively in his usage, Jesus presents positively.

Because of my education, I am aware of the theological distinctions and clarifications about what Jesus's words are supposed to mean: he is giving us his full Jesus-Christ self—that wonderful symbiosis of divinity and humanity. But the vehicle, the medium, and the final message here are physical, edible, chewable, yes, digestible human flesh. Much of ancient religion portrayed God eating or sacrificing humans or animals, which were offered on the altars, but Jesus turned religion and history on their heads, inviting us to imagine that God would give *himself as food for us!*

Further, some of us might know how to receive another human person. But God? This is a plunge that most cannot make early in their journeys, except perhaps in a highly intellectual way. In our hearts, we have a hard time believing we're worthy, which is probably why we create intellectual and moral reasons for disbelieving or excluding ourselves and others from the Eucharist. In the Roman Rite, we all publicly say before coming to the altar, "Lord, I am not worthy that you should come under my roof." Then those of us who come forward to receive are supposed to pretend that we are indeed worthy, it seems. And the message that everybody knows is that the "unworthy ones" (variously defined) should not come forward! A very mixed and contradictory message right in the heart of the liturgy.

One helpful piece of the Catholic ritual, however, is our orthodox belief in "Real Presence." By that we mean that Jesus is somehow physically present in the sacramental bread. This sets the stage for recipients to experience what I like to call "carnal knowledge" of God, who is normally assumed to be Spirit. It seems that mere mind-knowing is not enough, because it does not engage the heart or soul. The mistake happens when those who cannot make this mental assent are deemed "unworthy" to receive. But your only real prerequisite for participation or "worthiness" is in fact *your capacity for presence* yourself. This is not accomplished just in the head. Presence is a unique capacity that includes body, heart, mind, and whatever we mean by "soul." Love affairs never happen just in the mind.

Only presence can know presence. And our real presence can know Real Presence.

When Jesus spoke the words "This is my Body," I believe he was speaking not just about the bread right in front of him, but about the whole universe, about every thing that is physical, material, and yet also spirit-filled. (Thus the name of this book.) His assertion and our repetition resound over all creation before they also settle into one piece of bread. And you know what? The bread and wine, and all of creation, seem to believe who and what they are much more readily than humans do. They know they are the Body of Christ, even if the rest of us resist such a thought. When we speak these sacred words at the altar, we are speaking them to both the bread— and the congregation—so we can carry it "to all creation" (Mark 16:16). As St. Augustine said, we must feed the body of Christ to the people of God until they know that they are what they eat! And they are what they drink!

Honestly, and without any stretch, my dog Venus taught me more about "real presence" over a fifteen-year period than any theological manual ever did. Venus taught me how to be present to people and let them be present to me through the way she always sought out and fully enjoyed my company for its own sake. She was always so eager to be with me, even if I interrupted her in the middle of the night to go with me on a sick call. She literally modeled for me how to be present to God and how God must be present to me: "Like the eyes of a handmaid fixed on the hand of her mistress" (Psalm 123:2), Venus's eyes were always fixed on me. If only I could always have been as loyal, eager, and subservient to her. But she taught me how.

Presence is always reciprocal, or it is not presence at all.

The Universal Incarnate Presence

As if eating his body weren't enough, Jesus pushes us in even further and scarier directions by adding the symbolism of intoxicating wine as we lift the chalice and speak over all of suffering humanity, "This is my blood." Jesus then directs us, "Drink me, all of you!" Pause for a moment and try to step outside the domestication of the Eucharist that has occurred in the churches. Remember, contact with blood was usually ritual impurity for a Jew at that time. Is it just me, or is this beginning to have a Count Dracula feeling? Or is it supposed to? Is it supposed to be scandalous and shocking?

One of the things I've learned from studying male initiation rites is that startling, vivid rituals are the only ones that have much psychic effect—things like symbolic drowning, digging your own grave, rolling naked in ashes, or even the now outdated slap that the bishop used to give at Confirmation, which shock us into realization. Anything too tame has little psychic effect, at least for men, but I suspect for women too. There's a real difference between harmless repetitive ceremonies and life-changing rituals. *Scholars say that ceremonies normally confirm and celebrate the status quo and deny the shadow side of things (think of a Fourth of July parade), whereas true ritual offers an alternative universe, where the shadow is named (think of a true Eucharist). In the church, I am afraid we mostly have ceremonies.* Most masses I have ever attended are about affirming the status quo, which seldom reveals and often even denies the shadow side of church, state, or culture.

Many mystics and liberation theologians have further recognized that inviting us to drink wine *as his blood* is an invitation to live in bodily solidarity "with the blood of every person whose blood has been unjustly shed on this earth, from the blood of Abel the Holy to the blood of Zechariah" (Matthew 23:35). These are the first and last murders noted in the Hebrew Bible. In the act of drinking the blood of Christ at this Holy Meal, you are consciously uniting yourself with all unjust suffering in the world, from the beginning of time till its end. Wherever there was and is suffering, there is the sympathy and the empathy of God. "This is *all* my blood!" Jesus is saying, which sanctifies the victim and gives all bloodshed utter and final significance.

I think of this often as I pronounce these same words looking out over a congregation that barely seems interested in the message. *Seeing it as a miracle is not really the message at all.* I can see why we celebrate the Eucharist so often. This message is such a shock to the psyche, such a challenge to our pride and individualism, that it takes a lifetime of practice and much vulnerability for it to sink in—*as the pattern of every thing*—and not just this thing.

The bread and the wine together are stand-ins for *the very elements of the universe,* which also enjoy and communicate the incarnate presence. Why did we resist this message so much? Authentically Eucharistic churches should have been the first to recognize the corporate, universal, and physical nature of the "Christification" of matter. We must continue to offer humanity this wondrous homeopathic medicine, which feeds us *both the problem and its cure.* While Catholics rightly affirm the Real Presence of Jesus in these physical elements of the earth, most do not realize the implications of what they have affirmed. The bread and wine are largely understood as *an exclusive presence,* when in fact their full function is to communicate a truly inclusive—and always shocking—presence.

A true believer is eating what he or she is afraid to see and afraid to accept: *The universe is the Body of God, both in its essence and in its suffering.*

As Pope Francis insists, the Eucharistic bread and wine are not a prize for the perfect or a reward for good behavior. Rather they are food for the human journey and medicine for the sick. We come forward not because we are worthy but because we are all wounded and somehow "unworthy." "I did not come for the healthy, but for the sick," Jesus said (Mark 2:17). One wonders how we were so successful at missing this central point. God gives us our worthiness, and objectively so!

"Given for You"

The other momentous phrase that Jesus repeated at the Last Supper is the phrase "for you." In the accounts of Matthew, Mark, and Luke—and in Paul's too (1 Corinthians 11:24ff.)—Jesus says, my body "given for you," "broken for you," and my blood "poured out for you." Anyone who has ever enjoyed lovemaking knows that the thrill comes not just from the physical sensation but from the other person's desire to be specifically with *you*, to be naked *for you*, to delight *in you*, to pleasure *you*. You always want to say, "But why me?" And you hope the other says, "Because I love *you*!" It is the ultimate and very specific I-Thou experience of Martin Buber.

I was also told by a young woman on staff at our center that she believes women's menstrual cycles have given women, in particular, an experiential and cellular understanding of this experience. Because they shed blood monthly for the sake of life, and also give *blood and water* at birth, just as Jesus did on the cross (John 19:34). Of course! This "water and blood" had always struck me as strange symbolism. But maybe not for a woman, who knows the price of birth. How daring and shocking it was for Jesus to turn the whole tradition of impure blood on its heels and make blood *holy*—and even a point of contact with the divine! This deserves a whole book of commentary, and is supposed to be a stun-gun experience, which all true sacraments should be.

In the same way, mutual desiring is the intended impact of the Eucharist.

We know that Jesus loved to refer to himself as the "bridegroom" (John 3:29, Matthew 9:15), and one of his first recorded acts of ministry was whooping it up at a wedding feast (John 2:1), creating 150 gallons of wine out of water toward the end of the party! (What do Baptists do with that?) We also know that the very erotic *Song of Songs* somehow made its way into the Bible, and its images of union have been precious to mystics from the earliest centuries. Yet much of later Christianity has been rather prudish and ashamed of the human body, which God took on so happily through Jesus, and then gave away to us so freely in the Eucharist.

The Eucharist is an encounter of the heart, knowing Presence through our own offered presence. In the Eucharist, we move beyond mere words or rational thought and go to that place where we don't talk about the Mystery anymore; we begin to chew on it. Jesus did not say, "Think about this" or "Stare at this" or even "Worship this." Instead he said, "Eat this!"

We must move our knowing to the bodily, cellular, participative, and thus unitive level. We must keep eating and drinking the Mystery, until one day it dawns on us, in an undefended moment, "My God, I really am what I eat! I also am the Body of Christ." Then we can henceforth trust and allow what has been true since the first moment of our existence. As I mentioned before, the Eucharist should operate like a stun gun, not just a pretty ceremony. We have dignity and power flowing through us in our bare and naked existence—and everybody else does too, even though most do not know it. A body awareness of this sort is enough to steer and empower our entire faith life, while merely assenting to or saying the words will never give us the jolt we need *to absorb the divine desire for us—and for Itself.* Frankly, we're talking about the difference between receiving a sincere Valentine's Day card that says, "I love you," and making physical, naked, and tender love to someone you deeply care about and who cares for you. Why are we so afraid of that?

This is why I must hold to the orthodox belief that there is Real Presence in the bread and wine. For me, *if we sacrifice Reality in the elements, we end up sacrificing the same Reality in ourselves.* As Flannery O'Connor once declared: "Well, if it is just a symbol, to hell with it!"*

The Eucharist then becomes our ongoing touchstone for the Christian journey, a place to which we must repeatedly return in order to find our face, our name, our absolute identity, who we are in Christ, and thus who we are forever. *We are not just humans having a God experience. The Eucharist tells us that, in some mysterious way, we are God having a human experience!*

This continues in Romans 8:18–25 (as creation), 1 Corinthians 10:16ff. and 11:23ff. (as bread and wine), and in 12:12ff. (as people). In each of these Scriptures, and in an ever-expanding sense, Paul expresses his full belief that there is a real transfer of human and spiritual identity from Christ to Creation, to the elements of bread and wine, and through them to human beings. The Great Circle of Inclusion (the Trinity) is a centrifugal force that will finally pull everything back into itself—exactly as many physicists predict will happen to the universe the moment it finally stops expanding. They call it the "Big Crunch," and some even say it will take a nanosecond to happen. (Could this be a real description of the "Second Coming of Christ"? Or the "Final Judgment"? I think so.)

Thus Eucharist, like Resurrection, is not a unique event or strange anomaly.

---

* Flannery O'Connor, *The Habit of Being* (New York: Farrar, Straus and Giroux, 1979), 125.

Eucharist is the Incarnation of Christ taken to its final shape and end—the very elements of the earth itself.

It is all one continuum of Incarnation.

Who we are in God is who we all are.

Everything else is changing and passing away.

Written with great joy on Easter Sunday, 2017

12

Why Did Jesus Die?

Our predestination to glory is prior
by nature to any notion of sin.

—John Duns Scotus, OFM

Thirty-five years of men's work around the world have shown me how deeply the human psyche in almost every culture has been wounded and scarred by violent, unavailable, and abusive fathers and other men. The impact of this wounding on our spiritual sensitivities is profound. Of course, there is no shortage of reasons why someone wouldn't trust or believe in God, but surely one of the most counterproductive things Christians have done is add to those reasons by presenting "God the Father" as a tyrant, a sadist, a rage-aholic dad, or just an unreliable lover.

A clear case in point is the now-dominant explanation of why Jesus had to die and how that transaction is related to our salvation. It made God "the Father" distant and cold.

For most of Christian history, no single consensus prevailed on what it means when Christians say, "Jesus died for our sins," but in recent centuries one *theory* did take over. It was often referred to as the "penal substitutionary atonement theory," especially once it was developed after the Reformation. Substitutionary atonement is the theory that Christ, by his own sacrificial choice, was punished in the place of us sinners, thus satisfying the "demands of justice" so that God could forgive our sins. This theory of atonement ultimately relies on another commonly accepted notion—the "original sin" of Adam and Eve, which we were told taints all human beings. But much like original sin, which we considered earlier, most Christians have never been told how recent and regional this explanation is, and that it fully relies upon a retributive notion of justice. Nor are they told that it is just a theory, even though some groups take it as long-standing dogma. The early church never heard of this; at best they had some idea of "ransom" from the many biblical metaphors.

Until we see this explanation of why Jesus had to die for what it is and what it isn't, we'll struggle to liberate our notions of both Christ and Jesus and to see them as a revelation of the infinite love of the Trinity, not some bloody transaction "required" by God's offended justice in order to rectify the problem of human sin.

In this chapter, I hope to address how our commonly accepted atonement theory—especially as accomplished through the life, suffering, and death of Jesus—led to some serious misunderstandings of Jesus's role and Christ's eternal purpose, reaffirmed our narrow notion of retributive justice, and legitimated a notion of "good and necessary violence" all the way down. I take up this subject with both excitement and trepidation because I know the theory of substitutionary atonement is central to the faith of many. But the questions of *why Jesus died and what is the meaning and message of his death* have dominated the recent Christian narrative, often much more than his life and teaching. As some have said, if this theory is true, all we needed was the last three days or even three hours of Jesus's life. In my opinion, this interpretation has kept us from a deep and truly transformative understanding of both Jesus and Christ. Salvation became a *one-time transactional* affair between Jesus and his Father, instead of an ongoing *transformational lesson* for the human soul and for all of history.

At best, the theory of substitutionary atonement has inoculated us against the true effects of the Gospel, causing us to largely "thank" Jesus instead of honestly imitating him. At worst, it led us to see God as a cold, brutal figure, who demands acts of violence before God can love his own creation. Now, there is no doubt that both Testaments are filled with metaphors of atonement, sacrifice, expiation, ransom, paying the price, opening the gates, et cetera. But these are common temple metaphors that would've made sense to a Jewish audience. Anthropologically speaking, these words and assumptions reflect a magical or what I call "transactional" way of thinking. By that I mean that if you just believe the right thing, say the right prayer, or practice the right ritual, things will go right for you in the divine courtroom. In my experience, this way of thinking loses its power as people and cultures grow up and seek actual changes in their minds and hearts. Then, *transformational* thinking tends to supplant *transactional* thinking.

As I wrote earlier, Christianity's vision of God was a radical departure from most ancient religions. Instead of having God "eat" humans, animals, or crops, which are sacrificed on an altar, Christianity made the bold claim that God's very body was given *for us* to eat! *This turned everything around and undid the seeming logic of quid pro quo thinking.* As long as we employ any *retributive* notion of God's offended justice (required punishment for wrongdoing), we trade our distinctive Christian message for the cold, hard justice that has prevailed in most cultures throughout history. We offer no redemptive alternative to history but actually sanctify the very "powers and principalities" that Paul says unduly control the world

(Ephesians 3:9–10, 6:12). We stay inside of what some call the "myth of redemptive violence," which might just be the dominant story line of history.

It's time for Christianity to rediscover the deeper biblical theme of *restorative justice,* which focuses on rehabilitation and reconciliation and not punishment. (Read Ezekiel 16 for a supreme example of this.) We could call Jesus's story line the "myth of redemptive suffering"—not as in "paying a price" but as in offering the self for the other. Or "at-one-ment" instead of atonement!

Restorative justice, of course, comes to its full demonstration in the constant healing ministry of Jesus. Jesus represents the real and deeper level of teaching of the Jewish Prophets. Jesus never punished anybody! Yes, he challenged people, but always for the sake of insight, healing, and restoration of people and situations to their divine origin and source. Once a person recognizes that Jesus's mission (obvious in all four Gospels) was to heal people, not punish them, the dominant theories of retributive justice begin to lose their appeal and their authority.

The History of a Theory

It only makes sense that early Christians would look for a logical and deeply meaningful explanation for the "why" of the tragic death of their religion's founder. But for centuries, appeasing an angry, fanatical Father was not their answer. The consensus for the first eleven hundred years was that the sacrificial death of Jesus on the cross—the "price" or the ransom—was being paid not to God, but to the devil! Yes, I know this now seems silly, but it's what many Christians believed for almost a millennium. This made the devil pretty powerful and God pretty weak, but it gave the people someone to blame for Jesus's death. And at least it was not God at that point.

Then, in the eleventh century, Anselm of Canterbury wrote a paper called *Cur Deus Homo?* or "Why Did God Become a Human?" which, unfortunately, might just be the most successful piece of theology ever written. Thinking he could solve the problem of sin inside of the medieval code of feudal honor and shame, Anselm said, in effect, "Yes, a price did need to be paid to restore God's honor, and it needed to be paid to God the Father—by one who was equally divine." Apparently, Anselm never thought out the disastrous implications of his theory, especially for people who were already afraid or resentful of God. In authoritarian and patriarchal cultures, most people were fully programmed to think this way— working to appease an authority figure who was angry, punitive, and even violent in his reactions. Many still operate this way, especially if they had an angry or abusive parent. People respond to this kind of God because it fits their own story line.

Unfortunately, for a simple but devastating reason, this understanding also nullifies any in-depth spiritual journey: *Why would you love or trust or desire to be with such a God?*

Over the next few centuries, Anselm's honor- and shame-based way of thinking came to be accepted among Christians, though it met resistance from some, particularly my own Franciscan school. Protestants accepted the mainline Catholic position, and embraced it with even more fervor. Evangelicals later enshrined it as one of the "four pillars" of foundational Christian belief, which the earlier period would have thought strange. They were never told of the varied history of this belief, even among a few Protestants, and if you came from a full "law and order" culture, which most have till very recently, it made perfect sense.

The Franciscans, however, led by John Duns Scotus (1266–1308), refused to see the Incarnation, and its final denouement on the cross, as a mere reaction to sin. Instead, they claimed that the cross was a *freely chosen revelation of Total Love* on God's part. In so doing, they reversed the engines of almost all world religion up to that point, which assumed *we* had to spill blood to get to a distant and demanding God. On the cross, the Franciscan school believed, God was "spilling blood" to reach out to us!* This is a sea change in consciousness. The cross, instead of being a transaction, was seen as a dramatic demonstration of God's outpouring love, meant to utterly shock the heart and turn it back toward trust and love of the Creator.

In the Franciscan school, God did not need to be paid in order to love and forgive God's own creation for its failures. Love cannot be bought by some "necessary sacrifice"; if it could, it would not and could not work its transformative effects. Try loving your spouse or children that way, and see where it gets you. Scotus and his followers were committed to protecting *the absolute freedom and love of God*. If forgiveness needs to be bought or paid for, then it is not authentic forgiveness at all, which must be a free letting-go.

I'm not sure Christians even yet recognize the dangers of penal substitutionary atonement theory. Perhaps the underlying assumptions were never made clear, even though thinking people throughout the ages were often repelled by such a crass notion of God. Even more so in our time, these theories have become a nail in the coffin of belief for many. Some Christians just repress their misgiving because they think it implies a complete loss of faith. But I would wager that for every person who voices doubt, many more quietly walk away from a religion that has come to seem irrational, mythological, and deeply unsatisfying to the heart and soul. These are not bad people!

We can do so much better, and doing so will not diminish Jesus in the least. In fact, it will allow Jesus to take on a universal and

---

* Mary Beth Ingham, *Scotus for Dunces* (St. Bonaventure, NY: Franciscan Institute, 2003), 75ff.

humanly appealing dimension, striking at the heart of our inability to believe in unconditional love. The cross cannot be an arbitrary and bloody sacrifice entirely dependent on a sin that was once committed by one man and one woman under a tree between the Tigris and Euphrates rivers. That idea, frankly, reduces any notion of a universal or truly "catholic" revelation to one planet, at the edge of one solar system, in a universe of what now seem to be billions of galaxies, with trillions of solar systems. A religion based on necessary and required sacrifices, and those ending up required primarily of Jesus and later the underclass, is just not glorious enough for, hopeful enough for, or even befitting the marvelous creation that we are all a part of. To those who cling to Anselm's understanding, I would say, as J. B. Phillips wrote many years ago, "Your God is too small."

Far too many evils have been committed in history under the manipulative cry of "sacrifice," usually violent and necessary sacrifice for an always "noble" cause. (Just go to any Veterans Day parade and you'll see that sacrifice unites both liberals and conservatives rather quickly.) But I believe Jesus utterly undoes the very notion of *sacrificial requirements* for God to love us—first in himself, and then in all of us. "Go, learn the meaning of the words, what I want is mercy, not sacrifice!" Jesus said throughout the Gospels (Matthew 9:13, 12:7). He was quoting the prophet Hosea, who further added, "I want knowledge of God, not your holocausts" (6:6). Notions of sacrifice keep us in the retributive justice framework and outside of the essential Gospel of grace and undeserved love. This is major for understanding the Gospel. French philosopher and literary critic René Girard (1923–2015) goes to great length to demonstrate that Jesus puts to an end all notions of sacrificial religion, which only maintain our *quid pro quo* worldviews.* I highly recommend him.

---

* René Girard, *The Girard Reader,* ed. James G. Williams (New York: Crossroad, 1996).

A Collision of Cross-Purposes

With that for context, let me now offer you what I think is the first and most helpful meaning of Jesus's death—how the most famous act in Christian history both reveals the problem we are up against and gives us a way through it. My premise, as you'll see, is that:

It is not God who is violent. We are.

It is not that God demands suffering of humans. We do.

God does not need or want suffering—neither in Jesus nor in us.

Girard understands Hebrews's frequent "once and for all" language (7:27, 9:12, 26, 10:10) in a quite definitive way as the end of any need for any sacrifices by which to please God. The problem of divine love is settled forever from God's side. In our insecurity, we keep re-creating "necessary sacrifices."

Hear Jesus's words in John's Gospel: "I did not come to condemn the world, but to save it" (12:47). Or in Matthew, "Come to me all you who labor and are overburdened, and I will give you rest. . . . for I am gentle and humble of heart. Yes, my yoke is easy and my burden is light" (11:28). If you grew up a Christian, you've probably read verses like these dozens of times. But once you can make the switch from a juridical and punitive worldview to a grace-filled and transformative one, you will see such passages throughout the New Testament in a new and central light.

Most of us are still programmed to read the Scriptures according to the common laws of jurisprudence, which are hardly ever based on *restorative justice*. (Even the term was not common till recently.) Restorative justice was the amazing discovery of the Jewish prophets, in which Yahweh punished Israel by loving them even more! (Ezekiel 16:53ff.). Jurisprudence has its important place in human society, but it cannot be transferred to the divine mind. It cannot guide us inside the realm of infinite love or infinite anything. A worldview of weighing and counting is utterly insufficient

once you fall into the ocean of mercy. If I can ever so slightly paraphrase my dear Thérèse of Lisieux, *there is a science about which
God knows nothing—addition and subtraction.* Thérèse understood
the full and final meaning of being saved by grace alone as few have
in all of Christian history.

The Divine Mind transforms all human suffering by identifying
completely with the human predicament and standing in full solidarity with it from beginning to end. This is the real meaning of the
crucifixion. The cross is not just a singular event. It's a statement
from God that *reality has a cruciform pattern.* Jesus was killed in
a collision of cross-purposes, conflicting interests, and half-truths,
caught between the demands of an empire and the religious estab-
lishment of his day. The cross was the price Jesus paid for living in
a "mixed" world, which is both human and divine, simultaneously
broken and utterly whole. He hung between a good thief and a bad
thief, between heaven and earth, inside of both humanity and divinity, a male body with a feminine soul, utterly whole and yet utterly disfigured—all the primary opposites.

In so doing, Jesus demonstrated that Reality is not meaningless
and absurd, even if it isn't always perfectly logical or consistent.
Reality, we know, is always filled with contradictions, what St. Bonaventure and others (such as Alan of Lille and Nicholas of Cusa)
called the "coincidence of opposites."

Jesus the Christ, in his crucifixion and resurrection, "recapitu-
lated all things in himself, everything in heaven and everything on
earth" (Ephesians 1:10). This one verse is the summary of Franciscan Christology. Jesus agreed to carry the mystery of universal
suffering. He allowed it to change him ("Resurrection") and, it is to
be hoped, us, so that we would be freed from the endless cycle of
projecting our pain elsewhere or remaining trapped inside of it.

This is the fully resurrected life, the only way to be, happy, free,
loving, and therefore "saved." In effect, Jesus was saying, "If I can

trust it, you can too." We are indeed saved by the cross—more than we realize. The people who hold the contradictions and resolve them in themselves are the saviors of the world. They are the only real agents of transformation, reconciliation, and newness.

Christians are meant to be the visible compassion of God on earth more than "those who are going to heaven." They are the leaven who agree to share the fate of God for the life of the world now, and thus keep the whole batch of dough from falling back on itself. *A Christian is invited, not required to accept and live the cruciform shape of all reality.* It is not a duty or even a requirement as much as *a free vocation.* Some people feel called and agree to not hide from the dark side of things or the rejected group, but in fact draw close to the pain of the world and allow it to radically change their perspective. They agree to embrace the imperfection and even the injustices of our world, allowing these situations to change themselves from the inside out, which is the only way things are changed anyway.

As some of our saints have said in different ways, Jesus is not loyal to groups, to countries, to battles, to teams. *Jesus is loyal only to suffering.* He is as present to the suffering Iraqi soldier as he is to the wounded American soldier, as caring for the disillusioned Nazi warrior as for the discouraged British soldier bleeding to death in the field. As Isaiah shockingly puts it, "to him nations count as nothingness and emptiness" (40:17). The *Jesus Nation* crosses all boundaries and frontiers, and is occupied by only the wisdom and freedom of those who have suffered and come out the other side— not destroyed, but larger and stronger and wiser. The Gospel is simply the wisdom of those who agree to carry their part of the infinite suffering of God. Ironically, many non-Christians—I think of Anne Frank, Simone Weil, and Etty Hillesum, who were all Jewish— seemed to fully accept this vocation with greater freedom than many Christians.

Scapegoating, and the "Sin of the World"

For me, the Hebrew Scripture that most lays the foundation for understanding the death of Jesus is found in Leviticus 16, which French philosopher and historian René Girard calls the most effective religious ritual ever created. On the "Day of Atonement" the high priest Aaron was instructed to symbolically lay all the sins of the people on one unfortunate goat, and the people would then beat the animal until it fled into the desert. (The word "scapegoat" came from the phrase "escaping goat," used in early English translations of the Bible.) It was a vividly symbolic act that helped to unite and free the people in the short term. It foreshadowed what we Catholics would later call "general absolution" or "public confession." Instead of owning our sins, this ritual allowed us to export them elsewhere—in this case onto an innocent animal.

For our purposes here, the image of the scapegoat powerfully mirrors and reveals the universal, but largely unconscious, human need to transfer our guilt onto something (or someone) else by singling that other out for unmerited negative treatment. This pattern is seen in many facets of our society and our private, inner lives—so much so that you could almost name it "*the* sin of the world" (note that "sin" is singular in John 1:29). The biblical account, however, seems to recognize that only a "lamb of a God" can both *reveal and resolve* that sin in one nonviolent action. (Any *lion of a God* would perpetuate the illusion that we can overcome power with the same kind of power, only doubling the problem.)

Note too that the scapegoat in Leviticus is based on an arbitrary choice between two goats (Leviticus 16:7–10). There is really no difference between the "goat of YHWH, who is offered as a fitting sacrifice for sin" and the "goat of Azazel" (Azazel being a demon of the wastelands), who gets beaten into the desert—except in how the goat was seen and chosen by the people. Presumably God created both goats, but we humans are the ones who decide which should be driven out. Such dualistic thinking is not true, but our egos find it convenient and helpful—not to mention necessary for displacing blame.

To this day, scapegoating characterizes much personal, political, and public discourse. People on the Left accuse the Right of being merely "pro-birth" while being pro-war and pro-gun, and thus hypocritical when they call themselves "pro-life." People on the Right accuse the Left of being "pro-abortion" and "pro-choice," and thus not "pro-life" at all. By concentrating on the other group's goat, both sides can avoid being completely consistent. Amazing how this logic works quite effectively to keep both of us from being honest. In reality, a full and completely consistent pro-life position would probably please very few because of what it would demand—including the sacrifice of some of our unquestioned assumptions. Very few wear the "seamless garment" of being truly pro-life all the time. There is no completely pure place to stand, it seems, and before we can resolve an issue at any depth, we must honestly name and accept this imperfection. It is the egoic illusion of our own perfect rightness that often allows us to crucify others.

Girard demonstrated that the scapegoat mechanism is probably the foundational principle for the formation of most social groups and cultures. We seldom consciously know that we are scapegoating or projecting. As Jesus said, people literally "do not know what they are doing" (Luke 23:34). In fact, the effectiveness of this mechanism depends on *not* seeing it! It's almost entirely automatic, ingrained, and unconscious. "She made me do it." "He is guilty." "He deserves it." "They are the problem." "They are evil." Humans should recognize their own negativity and sinfulness, but instead we largely hate or blame almost anything else.

Unless scapegoating can be consciously seen and named through concrete rituals, owned mistakes, or what many call "re-

pentance," the pattern will usually remain unconscious and unchal-
lenged. It took until the twentieth century for modern psychology
to recognize how humans almost always project their unconscious
shadow material onto other people and groups, but Jesus revealed
the pattern two thousand years ago. "When anyone kills you, they
will think they are doing a holy duty for God," he said (John 16:2).
We hate our own faults in other people, and sadly we often find
the best cover for that projection in religion. God and religion, I am
afraid, have been used to justify most of our violence and to hide
from the shadow parts of ourselves that we would rather not admit.

Yet the scriptures rightly call such ignorant hatred and killing
"sin," and Jesus came precisely to "take away" (John 1:29) our capacity to commit it—by exposing the lie for all to see. Like talking with
any good spiritual director or confessor, gazing at the Crucified One
helps you see the lie in all its tragedy. Remember, Jesus stood as
the fully innocent one who was condemned by the highest authorities of both "church and state" (Rome and Jerusalem), an act that
should create healthy suspicion about how wrong even the highest
powers can be. Maybe power still does not want us to see this, and
that's why we concentrate so much on the private sins of the flesh.
The denied sins that are really destroying the world are much more
the sins that we often admire and fully accept in our public figures:
pride, ambition, greed, gluttony, false witness, legitimated killing,
vanity, et cetera. That is hard to deny.

As John puts it, "He will show the world how wrong it was about
sin, about who was really in the right, and about true judgment"
(16:8). This is what Jesus is exposing and defeating on the cross.
*He did not come to change God's mind about us. It did not need
changing. Jesus came to change our minds about God—and about
ourselves—and about where goodness and evil really lie.*

We Carry and Love What God Carries and Loves

What, then, does it mean to follow Jesus? I believe that we are invited to gaze upon the image of the crucified Jesus to soften our hearts toward all suffering, to help us see how we ourselves have been "bitten" by hatred and violence, and to know that God's heart has always been softened toward us. In turning our gaze to this divine truth—in dropping our many modes of scapegoating and self-justification—we gain compassion toward ourselves and all others who suffer. It largely happens on the psychic and unconscious level, but that is exactly where all of our hurts and our will to violence lie, lodged in the primitive "lizard brain," where we have almost no rational control.

A transformative religion must touch us at this primitive, brain-stem level, or it is not transformative at all. History is continually graced with people who somehow learned to act beyond and outside their self-interest and for the good of the world, people who clearly operated by a power larger than their own. The Gandhis of the world, the Oskar Schindlers, the Martin Luther King Jrs. Add to them Rosa Parks, Mother Teresa, Dorothy Day, Oscar Romero, Cesar Chavez, and many other "unknown soldiers." These inspiring figures gave us strong evidence that the mind of Christ still inhabits the world. Most of us are fortunate to have crossed paths with many lesser-known persons who exhibit the same presence. I can't say how one becomes such a person. All I can presume is that they all had their Christ moments, in which they stopped denying their own shadows, stopped projecting those shadows elsewhere, and agreed to own their deepest identity in solidarity with the world.

But it is not an enviable position, this Christian thing.

Following Jesus is a vocation to share the fate of God for the life of the world.

To allow what God for some reason allows—and uses.

And to suffer ever so slightly what God suffers eternally.

Often, this has little to do with believing the right things about God—beyond the fact that God is love itself.

Those who agree to carry and love what God loves—which is both the good and the bad—and to pay the price for its reconciliation within themselves, these are the followers of Jesus Christ. They are the leaven, the salt, the remnant, the mustard seed that God uses to transform the world. The cross, then, is a very dramatic image of what it takes to be *usable* for God. It does not mean you are going to heaven and others are not; rather, it means you have entered into heaven much earlier and thus can see things in a transcendent, whole, and healing way now.

To maintain this mind and heart over the long haul is true spirituality. I have no doubt that it takes many daily decisions and many surrenders. It is aided by seeking out like-minded people. Such grace and freedom is never a lone achievement. A heaven you created by yourself will never be heaven for long. Saints are those who wake up while in this world, instead of waiting for the next one. Francis of Assisi, William Wilberforce, Thérèse of Lisieux, and Harriet Tubman did not feel superior to anyone else; they just knew they had been let in on a big divine secret, and they wanted to do their part in revealing it.

They all refused to trust even their own power unless that power had first been taught and refined by powerlessness.

This is no easy truth. Once their entire frame of mind had been taken apart and reshaped in this way, they had to figure out how they fit back into the dominant worldview—and most of them never did, at least not completely. This became their crucifixion. The "way of the cross" can never go out of style because it will surely never be *in* style. It never becomes the dominant consciousness anywhere. But this is the powerlessness of God, the powerlessness that saves the world.

The scapegoat mechanism, our ability to hate ourselves in others and attack, is too seductive and too difficult for most people to recognize. It must be opposed anew by every generation and every culture. The Kingdom of God is always a leaven, a remnant, a critical mass, a few chosen ones, a Jewish minyan—"ten just men"—who save us from ourselves for the sake of truth.

God is the ultimate nonviolent one, so we dare not accept any theory of salvation that is based on violence, exclusion, social pressure, or moral coercion. When we do, these are legitimated as a proper way of life. *God saves by loving and including, not by excluding or punishing.*

This God is calling *every one and every thing, not just a few chosen ones,* to God's self (Genesis 8:16–17, Ephesians 1:9–10, Colossians 1:15–20, Acts 3:21, 1 Timothy 2:4, John 3:17). To get every one and every thing there, God first needs models and images who are willing to be "conformed to the body of his death" and transformed into the body of his resurrection (Philippians 3:10). These are the "new creation" (Galatians 6:15), and their transformed state is still seeping into history and ever so slowly transforming it into "life and life more abundantly" (John 10:10).

If we do not recognize that we ourselves are the problem, we will continue to make God the scapegoat—which is exactly what we did by the killing of the God-Man on the cross. The crucifixion of Jesus—whom we see as the Son of God—was a devastating prophecy that humans would sooner kill God than change themselves. Yet the God-Man suffers our rejection willingly so something bigger can happen.

A Dialogue with the Crucified God

Many years ago, I wrote a meditation that I called "A Dialogue with the Crucified God," to help people experience what I am so feebly trying to describe here. I suggest you wait until you have an open, quiet, and solitary slot of time, then pray it out loud so your ears can hear your own words from your own mouth. In addition, I suggest that you place yourself before a tender image of the crucified Jesus that will allow you to both give and receive.

And know two things before you begin:

- We need images to reveal inner states. You are going to look at an image of what humans deny and are most afraid of: exposure, shame, vulnerability, and failure. Like a homeopathic medicine, Jesus became the problem on full display—to free us from that very problem. The cross withdraws the curtain of both denial and fear from our eyes and from our psyches. Jesus became the victim so we could stop victimizing others or playing the victim ourselves.

- Any authentic image of the crucified one is already an image of resurrection. The open arms and the knowing gaze are already the victory over any suffering.

JESUS SPEAKS TO YOU FROM THE CROSS

I am what you are most afraid of: your deepest, most wounded, and naked self. I am what you do to what you could love.

I am your deepest goodness and your deepest beauty,

which you deny and disfigure. Your only badness consists in what you do to goodness—your own and anybody else's.

You run away from, and you even attack, the only thing that will really transform you. But there is nothing to hate or to attack. If you try, you will become a mirror image of the same.

Embrace it all in me. I am yourself. I am all of creation. I am everybody and every thing.

YOU SPEAK BACK TO THE CRUCIFIED ONE

Brother Jesus, you are my life, which I deny. You are my death, which I fear. I embrace them both in you. Now I recognize—through you and because of you—that death and life are not opposites. You are my full self—exposed. You are infinite in action, which makes me infinite in becoming. This is my divine possibility. (*Stay with this thought until it moves beyond words.*)

You, Brother Jesus, are my outrageously ignored and neglected soul. You are what we do to goodness. You are what we do to God. You are the outrageously ignored and neglected soul of every thing. You are what we do to what we should and could love. You are what we do to one another. You are what we do to the Reality right in front of us. You are what we do to ourselves. (*Stay with this until it sinks in.*)

I hate and fear the very things that will save me. May this thought help me to love these things, be patient with them, and even forgive them.

I just cannot let anybody love me "for nothing." I insist on being worthy and deserving. And then I demand the same of others too. Yet your arms remain outstretched and embracing to all the world.

You alone, Christ Jesus, refuse to be a crucifier, even at the cost of being crucified. You never play the victim or call for any vengeance, but only breathe a universal forgiveness upon the universe from this crucified place—your upside-down throne.

We humans so often hate ourselves, but we mistakenly kill you and others instead.

You always knew we would do this, didn't you? And you accepted it.

Now you invite me out of this endless cycle of illusion and violence toward myself and toward anybody else.

I want to stop crucifying your blessed flesh, this blessed humanity, this holy mother earth.

I thank you, Brother Jesus, for becoming a human being and walking the full journey with me. Now I do not have to pretend that I am God.

This is more than enough and more than good, just to know we are doing it together.

I thank you for becoming finite and limited, so I do not have to pretend that I am infinite or limitless.

I thank you for becoming small and inferior, so I do not have to pretend that I am big and superior to anybody.

I thank you for holding our shame and nakedness so boldly and so publicly, so I do not need to hide or deny our human reality.

I thank you for accepting exclusion and expulsion, being crucified "outside the walls" and allowing me to know that I will meet you exactly there.

I thank you for "becoming sin," so I do not need to deny

my own failures, and can recognize that even my mistakes are the truest and most surprising path to love.

I thank you for becoming weak, so I do not have to pretend to be strong.

I thank you for being willing to be considered imperfect, wrong, and strange, so I do not have to be perfect or right, or idealize the so-called normal.

I thank you for not being loved or liked by so many, so I do not have to try so hard to be loved and liked by anybody.

I thank you for being considered a failure, so I do not have to pretend or even try to be a "success."

I thank you for allowing yourself to be considered wrong by the standards of both state and religion, so I do not have to be right anywhere.

I thank you for being poor in every way, so I do not have to seek being rich in any way.

I thank you, Brother Jesus, for being all of the things that humanity despises and fears, so I can fully accept myself—and everyone else—in and through you!

Crucified Jesus, I thank you for revealing all these things to me in one great image of insight and mercy. Yes, what the medieval mystics said is true, *Crux probat omnia*—"The cross legitimates/proves/uses everything." *(Stay with this Christian maxim until it make sense to you.)*

I want to love you in this form, Brother Jesus. I need to love you in this way, or I will never be free or happy in this world.

You and I, Brother Jesus, we are the same.

13

It Can't Be Carried Alone

*There is one Body, one Spirit, and you were all called
into one and the same hope. . . .
And each one of us has been given his own
share of grace, as Christ allotted it.*
—Ephesians 4:4, 7

For the last few years, I have had to stop watching the evening news because I could not bear to see any more women and children running for their lives in Syria or babies starving in Africa. It all made me deeply heartsick and even nauseous. I did not like being human. Then my country entered into an election cycle where words seemed to lose all meaning. It was about illusion and naked ambition on all sides. American politics felt vacuous, delusional, empty—and thus vain—a foundation on which it's impossible to build a civilization. And yet large numbers, including 82 percent of white Evangelicals and 52 percent of white Catholics, seemed to think blatant racism and rather universal mean-spiritedness were somehow like the

Jesus they loved so much. My heart ached for something solid and real. How could this be happening?

Then, days before I began writing this book, I learned that I would have to put down my fifteen-year-old black Lab because she was suffering from an inoperable cancer. Venus had been giving me a knowing and profoundly accepting look for weeks, but I did not know how to read it. Deep down, I did not want to know. After her diagnosis, every time I looked at her, she gazed up at me with those same soft and fully permissive eyes, as if to say, "It is okay, you can let me go. I know it is my time." But she patiently waited until I too was ready.

I cried off and on for a month after Venus's death, especially when I saw another dog, or pronounced her name. But in those weeks before she died, Venus *somehow* communicated to me that all sadness, whether cosmic, human, or canine, is one and the same. Somehow, her eyes were all eyes, even God's eyes, and the sadness she expressed was a divine and universal sadness. I wondered if God might have an easier time using animals to communicate who God is, since they do not seem as willful and devious as we are. Still, I thought, was this all a projection, a mere product of sentiment and imagination?

A short time later, these ideas crystallized for me while I was on retreat writing this book. A friend had dropped off a DVD of the critically acclaimed movie *Lion*, thinking I needed a break from my work. Grudgingly, I gave in to some lowly entertainment! As I followed the heartbreaking, true story of an East Indian boy and his lifelong search for himself and his family, my sadness reached a tipping point, and I began heaving with tears. The lament "Life is so unfair" overwhelmed me! There, in the solitude of my retreat, I fell into a kind of deep despair. Nothing meant anything for hours and into days. I just wanted off the boat of humanity.

In that moment, I was not sad about any one thing, but about everything. The tragedies I had witnessed in the previous months all piled up and overflowed into one big, clumped-together sadness and suffering that I couldn't escape. It is what my friend William Paul Young calls the "Great Sadness," a pain so huge and so deep, it feels as though it will never end. And yet the sadness was focused not on one particular issue but on all of them at once.

For me, and I can only say for me, it deeply helped to think back to Venus's eyes, and name all of this suffering and sadness as *the one sadness of God*. Then I did not have to hold it alone. And I learned I could not hold it alone, but it was a shared experience—which gave me great consolation. In some deeply illogical and non-rational way, I identified with what Paul writes at the beginning of Colossians: "It makes me happy to suffer for you, as I am suffering now, and in my own body to do what I can to make up all that still has to be undergone by Christ" (Colossians 1:24).

I am no masochist, and I surely have no martyr complex, but I do believe that the only way out of deep sadness is to go *with it* and *through it*. Sometimes I wonder if this is what we mean when we lift up the chalice of wine at the Eucharist and say, "Through him, with him, and in him." I wonder if the only way to spiritually hold suffering—and not let it destroy us—is to recognize that we cannot do it alone. When I try to heroically do it alone, I slip into distractions, denials, and pretending—and *I do not learn suffering's softening lessons*. But when I can find a shared meaning for something, especially if it allows me to love God and others in the same action, God can get me through it. I begin to trust the ambiguous process of life.

When we carry our small suffering in solidarity with the one universal longing of all humanity, it helps keep us from self-pity or self-preoccupation. We know that we are all in this together, and it is just as hard for everybody else. *Almost all people are carrying a great and secret hurt, even when they don't know it.* When we can make the shift to realize this, it softens the space around our overly defended hearts. It makes it hard to be cruel to anyone. It somehow makes us one—in a way that easy comfort and entertainment never can.

Some mystics even go so far as to say that individual suffering doesn't exist at all—and that there is only one suffering, it is all the same, and it is all the suffering of God. The image of Jesus on the cross somehow communicates that to the willing soul. A Crucified God is the dramatic symbol of *the one suffering* that God fully enters into *with us*—much more than just *for us,* as we were mostly trained to think.

If suffering, even unjust suffering (and all suffering is unjust), is part of one Great Mystery, then I am willing—and even happy sometimes—to carry my little portion. But I must know that it is somehow helping someone or something, and that it matters in the great scheme of things. Etty Hillesum, whom we met earlier, truly believed her suffering was also the suffering of God. She even expressed a deep desire to help God carry some of it. Such freedom and such generosity of spirit are almost unimaginable to me. What creates such larger-than-life people? Their altruism is hard to understand by almost any psychological definition of the human person.

"One Lump"

In the fourteenth century, the inspired, anonymous author of *The Cloud of Unknowing* taught that God in Christ dealt with sin, death, forgiveness, salvation *"all in one lump."* It is a most unusual, even homely phrase, but for me, this corporate and even mystical reading of divine history contributes toward the unitive vision we are seeking, as we try to understand the Universal Christ. Jesus by himself looks like an individual, albeit a divine individual, but the Christ I have described in this book is a compelling image for this "one-lump" view of reality. In the fourteenth century, the book's author would've enjoyed the last remnants of mystical holism before it was taken away by the dualistic—but also necessary—ravages of the Reformation and the Enlightenment. He reflected the more Eastern church understanding *of the resurrection as a universal phenomenon,* and not just the lone Jesus rising from the dead and raising his hands as if he just scored a touchdown, as is depicted in most Western art—and even in a giant mosaic that looms over the University of Notre Dame's football stadium. ("Touchdown Jesus," we used to call it.)

I am convinced that the Gospel offers us a holistic, "all in one lump" understanding of things. Once you have a similar breakthrough, you will see this idea everywhere in Pauline passages, expressed in different ways: "in that one body he condemned sin" (Romans 8:3); "He experienced death for all humankind" (Hebrews 2:19); he has done suffering and sacrifice "once and for all" (Hebrews 7:28); or the embodiment language of Philippians, where Jesus is said to lead us through the "pattern of sin and death" so we can "take our place in the pattern of resurrection" (3:9–12). And of course, this all emerges from Jesus's major metaphor of the "Reign of God," a fully collective notion, which some scholars say is just about all that he talks about. Until we start reading the Jesus story through the collective notion that the Christ offers us, I honestly think we miss much of the core message, and read it all in terms of individual salvation, and individual reward and punishment. Society will remain untouched.

I think this collective notion is what Christians were trying to verbalize when they made a late addition to the ancient Apostles' Creed, "I believe in the communion of saints." They were offering us this new idea that the dead are at one with the living, whether they're our direct ancestors, the saints in glory, or even the so-called souls in purgatory. The whole thing is one, just at different stages, all of it loved corporately by God (and, one hopes, by us). Within this worldview, we are saved not by being privately perfect, but by being "part of the body," humble links in the great chain of history. This view echoes *the biblical concept of a covenant love that was granted to Israel as a whole,* and never just to one individual like Abraham, Noah, or David. This is absolutely clear in the text; and to ignore it is to miss a major and crucial message. Christians as late as the 1500s still saw it that way, but I cannot imagine us adding such a statement to the creed in today's religious landscape. We are now too preoccupied with the "salvation of individuals" to read history in a corporate way, and the results have been disastrous. The isolated individual is now left fragile and defensive, adrift in a huge ocean of others who are also trying to save themselves—and not the whole. Christianity is now more of a contest, or even an ego trip, than a proclamation of divine victory and love.

I suspect that Western *individualism* has done more than any other single factor to anesthetize and even euthanize the power of the Gospel. Salvation, heaven, hell, worthiness, grace, and eternal life all came to be read through the lens of the separate ego, crowding God's transformative power out of history and society. Even Martin Luther's needed "justification by faith" sent us on a five-hundred-year battle for the private soul of the individual.* Thus leaving us with almost no care for the earth, society, the outsider, or the full Body of Christ. This is surely one reason why Christianity found itself incapable of critiquing social calamities like Nazism, slavery, and Western consumerism. For five hundred years, Christian teachers defined and redefined salvation almost entirely in in-

---

* See Krister Stendahl, "The Apostle Paul and the Introspective Conscience of the West." *The Harvard Theological Review* 56, no. 3 (1963): 199–215.

dividualistic terms, while well-disguised social evils—greed, pride, ambition, deceit, gluttony—moved to the highest levels of power and influence, even in our churches.

The lone individual is far too small and insecure to carry either the "weight of glory" or the "burden of sin" on his or her own. Yet that is the impossible task we gave the individual. It will never work. It creates well-disguised religious egocentricity, because we are forced to take our single and isolated selves far too seriously— *both our wonderfulness and our terribleness*—which are both their own kinds of ego trips, I am afraid.

One side effect of our individualized reading of the Gospel is that it allows the clergy great control over individual behavior, via threats and rewards. Obedience to authorities became the highest virtue in this framework, instead of love, communion, or solidarity with God or others, including the marginalized.

We recognized hierarchical or vertical accountability but *almost no lateral accountability to one another*—as Jesus hoped for the world when he prayed that we "all might be one" (John 17:21). A corporate reading of the Gospel gives hope and justice to history, but less control over individuals, which is probably why clergy who do the preaching don't like it too much and thus don't preach it too much.

I saw this in my own experience of pre–Vatican II Catholicism and seminary. In those days, I'm afraid, the only admired and promoted virtues were *obedience and loyalty to the church*. No one taught us how to love very well, or to be loyal to humanity as a whole—at least from the pulpit. Nor were most of my professors very loving men, if I would be honest. They were often ordained because they could pass academic tests, not because they were pastors or prophets or people people. They were trained to be joiners, believers, and loyalists more than servants of the mystery of God. Churchmen more than Gospel men. Conformity is not the same as love; joining does not imply an actual change of heart and mind. Few taught us how to be the Sympathy of God or Compassion for the World, and this experience has seemed true in varying degrees in every denomination I have worked with.

Unless we find the *communal meaning and significance* of the suffering of all life and ecosystems on our planet, we will continue to retreat into our individual, small worlds in our quest for personal safety and sanity. *Privatized salvation never accumulates into corporate change because it attracts and legitimates individualists to begin with.* Think about that.

One Life, One Death, One Suffering

The Universal Christ is trying to communicate at the deepest intuitive level that there is only One Life, One Death, and One Suffering on this earth. We are all invited to ride the one wave, which is the only wave there is. Call it Reality, if you wish. But we are all in this together.

Consider how a "one-lump" awareness of reality upends so many of our current religious obsessions. Our arguments about private worthiness; reward and punishment; gender, race, and class distinctions; private possessions, all the things that make us argue and compete, largely become a waste of time and an illusion. All these lived arguments depend on some type of weighing, measuring, counting, listing, labeling, and comparing. The Gospel, by contrast, is about learning to live and die *in and with* God—all our warts included and forgiven by an Infinite Love. The true Gospel democratizes the world.

We are all saved in spite of our mistakes and in spite of ourselves.

We are all caught up in the cosmic sweep of Divine grace and mercy.

And we all must learn to trust the Psalmist's prayer: "Not to us, not to us, O Lord, but to your name be the glory" (Psalm 115:1).

The freeing, good news of the Gospel is that God is saving and redeeming the Whole first and foremost, and we are all caught up in this Cosmic Sweep of Divine Love. The parts—you and me and everybody else—are the blessed beneficiaries, the desperate hangers-on, the partly willing participants in the Whole. Paul wrote that our only task is to trust this reality "until God is all in all" (1 Corinthians 15:28). What a different idea of faith! "When Christ is revealed," Paul writes to the Colossians, "and he is your life—you too will be revealed in all your glory with him" (3:4). Unless and until we can enjoy this, so much of what passes for Christianity will amount to little more than well-disguised narcissism and self-referential politics. We see this phenomenon playing out in the de facto values of people who strongly identify as Christian. Often they are more racist, classist, and sexist than non-Christians. "Others can carry the burden and the pain of injustice, but not my group," they seem to say.

Once I know that all suffering is both *our suffering and God's suffering,* I can better endure and trust the desolations and disappointments that come my way. I can live with fewer comforts and conveniences when I see my part in global warming. I can speak with a soft and trusting voice in the public domain if doing so will help lessen human hatred and mistrust. I can stop circling the wagons around my own group, if doing so will help us recognize our common humanity.

If I can recognize that all suffering and crucifixion (divine, planetary, human, animal) is "one body" and will one day be transmuted into the "one body" of cosmic resurrection (Philippians 3:21), I can at least live without going crazy or being permanently depressed. In this same passage, Paul goes on in this verse to say that "God will do this by the same power ['operation' or 'energy'] by which he is transforming the whole universe." It is all one continuous movement for him. We must point out these almost hidden but fully corporate understandings in Paul, since most Western dualistic minds have been preconditioned to read his letters in a purely anthropocentric and individualistic way. This is neither good nor new. It is the same old story line of secular society with some religious frosting on top.

Our full "Christ Option"—and it is indeed a free choice to jump on board—offers us so much that is both good and new—*a God who is in total solidarity with all of us at every stage of the journey, and who will get us all to our destination together in love.*

It is no longer about being correct. It is about being connected. Being in right relationship is much, much better than just trying to be "right."

14

The Resurrection Journey

Everything will be all right in the end.
If it's not all right, it is not yet the end.
—*The Best Exotic Marigold Hotel*

We've been talking about how suffering and sadness can take on a positive meaning when we shift to a "one-lump" view of reality. But if all of us are one in suffering, wouldn't we also need to say that we're one in life too? In this chapter I want to enlarge your view of resurrection—from a one-time miracle in the life of Jesus that asks for assent and belief, to a pattern of creation that has always been true, and that invites us to much more than belief in a miracle. It must be more than the private victory of one man to prove that he is God.

No preacher or teacher ever pointed this out to me, but in Paul's discourse to the Corinthians on the nature of resurrection, he says something very different from what most of us hear or expect. Paul writes, "If there is no resurrection from death, Christ himself cannot have been raised" (1 Corinthians 15:13). He presents "resurrection" as a universal principle, but most of us only remember the following verse: "If Christ has not been raised, our preaching is useless, and your faith is useless" (15:14). Verse 14 gives us a good apologetic statement about Jesus's resurrection, but the preceding verse strongly implies that the reason we can trust Jesus's resurrection is *that we can already see resurrection happening everywhere else.* Why didn't we see that? Maybe it is because only modern science now makes it apparent?

If the universe is "Christened" from the very beginning, then of course it can never die forever.

Resurrection is just incarnation taken to its logical conclusion.

If God inhabits matter, then we can naturally believe in the "resurrection" of the body.

Most simply said, *nothing truly good can die!* (Trusting that is probably our real act of faith!)

Resurrection is presented by Paul as the general principle of all reality. He does not argue from a one-time anomaly and then ask us to believe in this Jesus "miracle," which most Christians are eager to do. Instead, Paul names the cosmic pattern, and then says in many places that the "Spirit carried in our hearts" is the icon, the guarantee, the pledge, and the promise, or even the "down payment" of that universal message (see 2 Corinthians 1:21–22, Ephesians 1:14). Like I am feebly trying to do in this whole book, he is always grabbing for metaphors that will bring the universal message home.

Nothing is the same forever, says modern science. Ninety-eight percent of our bodies' atoms are replaced every year. Geologists with good evidence over millennia can prove that no landscape is permanent. Water, fog, steam, and ice are all the same thing, but at different stages and temperatures. *"Resurrection" is another word for change, but particularly positive change—which we tend to see only in the long run. In the short run, it often just looks like death.* The Preface to the Catholic funeral liturgy says, "Life is not ended, it is merely changed." Science is now giving us a very helpful language for what religion rightly intuited and imaged, albeit in mythological language. Remember, *myth* does not mean "not true," which is the common misunderstanding; it actually refers to things that are *always true*!

God could not wait for modern science to give history hope. It was enough to believe that Jesus "was raised from the dead," somehow planting the hope and possibility of resurrection in our deepest unconscious. Jesus's first incarnate life, his passing over into death, and his resurrection into the ongoing Christ life is the archetypal model for the entire pattern of creation. He is the microcosm for the whole cosmos, or the map of the whole journey, in case you need or want one. Nowadays most folks do not seem to think they need that map, especially when they are young. But the vagaries and disappointments of life's journey eventually make you long for some overall direction, purpose, or goal beyond getting through another day.

All who hold any kind of unexplainable hope believe in resurrection, whether they are formal Christians or not, and even if they don't believe Jesus was physically raised from the dead. I have met such people from all kinds of backgrounds, religious and nonreligious. I do, however, believe in the physical resurrection of Jesus, because it affirms what the whole physical and biological universe is also saying—and grounds it as something more than a mere spiritual or miraculous belief. It must also be a fully practical and material belief! If matter is inhabited by God, then matter is somehow eternal, and when the creed says, we believe in the "resurrection of the body," it means our bodies too and not just Jesus's body! As in him, so also in all of us. As in all of us, so also in him. So I am quite conservative and orthodox by most standards on this important issue, although I also realize it seems to be a very different kind of embodiment from all of the resurrection accounts in the Gospels. I believe in "a new heaven and a new earth" (Isaiah 65:17, Romans 8:18–25, 2 Peter 3:13, Revelation 21:1); and I believe *the resurrection of Jesus is like the icon you click on your computer to get to the right place.*

Christianity's true and unique story line has always been incarnation. If creation is "very good" (Genesis 1:34) at its very inception, how could such a divine agenda ever be undone by any human failure to fully cooperate? "Very good" sets us on a trajectory toward resurrection, it seems to me. God does not lose or fail. That is what it means to be God.

Jesus and Christ are both the CliffsNotes read on Reality for those of us who do not have time or mind to analyze the whole situation by ourselves. And who does in one small lifetime?

The Wedding Banquet

Jesus's most consistent metaphor and image for this final state of affairs was some version of a wedding feast or banquet.* In all four Gospels, Jesus refers to himself as the host, or "bridegroom," for an open and inclusive banquet, available to "good and bad alike" (Matthew 22:10). He seemed to know that people would not naturally like that, however. So there is already pushback included in the text: guests angling for a higher place at the table (Luke 14:7–11), hosts insisting that all the guests wear wedding garments (Matthew

---

* See Matthew 8:11, 22:2ff.; Luke 13:29, 14:15ff.; and Revelation 19:9. All those passages draw on the source texts of Isaiah 25:6–12 and 55:1–5.

22:11–14), or wanting to offer the wonderful event only to those "who could pay them back" while rejecting "the poor, the crippled, the lame, and the blind" (Luke 14:12–14). We have always made it hard for God to give away God—for free!

The fragile ego always wants to set a boundary, a price, an entrance requirement of some sort. Many Christians sadly prefer to read these passages from a worldview of scarcity instead of the Gospel of divine abundance, and this constant resistance to Infinite Love is revealed in the biblical text itself. The problem is tied up with the solution, as it were, the pushback included in the resolution.* There seems to be a necessary villain in every story line, and the villain is almost always found inside the biblical text. I know no other way to make sense of the Bible's many obvious contradictions and inconsistencies about God.

The ungenerous mind does not like the wedding banquet. It prefers a dualistic courtroom scene as its metaphor for the end of time, which is why Matthew 25's sheep and goats are the end-times parable that most people remember, even though they do not follow its actual message about care for the poor, and remember only the scary verdict at the end. In other words, Matthew 25:46b is allowed to trump all of Matthew 25:31–45. Scared people remember threats and do not hear invitations!

Just as the first creation of something out of nothing (*creatio ex nihilo*) seems impossible to the human mind, so any notion of life after death seems to demand the same huge leap of faith. Grace's foundational definition could be "something coming from nothing," and the human mind just does not know how to process that. Just as it does not like grace, it does not like resurrection. It is the same

---

* John Dominic Crossan, *How to Read the Bible and Still Be a Christian* (New York: HarperCollins, 2018). Here this same point is made in a much more detailed and scholarly fashion than I can.

resistance. Resurrection, like most gifts of goodness, is also a *creatio ex nihilo,* which is precisely God's core job description: God is the one *"who gives life to the dead and calls into existence the things that do not exist"* (Romans 4:17b), according to a wonderful line from Paul. Or as Walt Whitman so beautifully put it:

> *All goes onward and outward . . . and nothing collapses,*
> *And to die is different from what any one supposed,*
> *and much luckier.**

"Reality with a Personality"

The central issue here is not whether Jesus did or did not physically rise from the dead, which supposedly "proves" the truth of the Christian religion if you agree, and disproves it if you disagree. No scientific proof is ever likely to be possible. Besides, our endless attempts to prove a supernatural event are misguided from the start, because neither Christ nor Jesus is *outside of our natural reality* in the first place.

It will really help you, Christian or not, if you can begin to see Jesus—and Christ—as coming out of Reality, naming it, giving it a face, not appearing to Reality from another world. There is no group to join here, no need to sign on the dotted line, only a generous moment of recognition that the Inner and the Outer are one and the same. Our inner meaning and Christ's outer meaning, if you will. They mirror one another: Human anthropology matches a divine theology. How is that for one Great Ecosystem? If one's theology (view of God) does not significantly change one's anthropology (view of humanity), it is largely what we call a "head trip."

---

*   Walt Whitman, "A child said, What is the grass," in *Song of Myself,* 6.

Resurrection is also grace taken to its logical and full conclusion. If reality begins in grace, it of course must continue "grace upon grace" (John 1:16b) and "from this fullness we have all received" (1:16a). In such a field, we now might have the courage to join Jesus in imagining that "I and the Father are one" (John 10:30) too. That is what I mean by theology changing anthropology. If death and resurrection are just about Jesus, and not about history, the world will continue to lose interest in our story line.

The evolutionary theologian Michael Dowd loves to say that God might best be seen as *"Reality with a personality."** Through God, the world around us—everything that is—seems to be in dialogue with us, whether we enjoy it or not, whether we trust it or not. I hope that is as helpful to you as it is to me. Even when our lives feel meaningless, we can still trust and be confident that Someone is talking, and that Someone is also listening when we talk. To be outside of that constant interface is probably what it means to *not* believe. Every time you choose love or positively connect with someone or something, you are in touch with the Divine Personality. You do not even need to call it "God"—God does not seem to care at all. It is equally important to say that to negatively connect, to hate, fear, or oppose, is *not* to meet the Divine Personality. Thus we are strongly warned against such negativity in every way, and such things are called "sin" or even the state of "hell," which is not really a geographical place but a very real state of consciousness. All rewards and punishments must primarily be seen as first of all now—*and inherent in good and bad behavior.*

It is very interesting to me that the New Testament only "sends out" those *(apostolos)* who can be "witnesses to resurrection" (Luke 24:48, Acts 1:22, 3:15b, 13:31), that is, witnesses to this immense

---

* Michael Dowd, *Thank God for Evolution* (New York: Viking, 2007), 118ff. A really brilliant, life-changing book.

inner and outer conversation that is always going on. Otherwise, we have little to say that is really helpful, and we just create unnecessary problems for people. Negative or cynical people, conspiracy theorists, and all predictors of Armageddon are the polar opposites of witnesses to resurrection. And many such people appear to be running the world and even the churches. The Christ of John's Gospel says, "Be brave. I have overcome the world" (16:33) and its hopelessness. Courage and confidence is our message! Not threat and fear.

What Happened at Jesus's Resurrection?

What happened at the resurrection is that Jesus was fully revealed as the eternal and deathless Christ in embodied form. Basically, *one circumscribed body of Jesus morphed into ubiquitous Light.* Henceforth, light is probably the best metaphor for Christ or God.

For most of the first six centuries, the moment of Jesus's resurrection was deemed unpaintable or uncarvable. The custom for a long time was just to picture the shrine in Jerusalem where the resurrection was supposed to have happened—but never the event itself.* Similarly, the event is not even described as such in the New Testament. All we see are the aftermath stories—stunned guards, seated angels, and visiting women. The closest thing we have to an immediate description is indirectly given in Matthew 27:51–53, but this describes a general resurrection of tombs opening and bodies rising, and not just the raising up of Jesus. Read this verse now, and

---

* John Dominic Crossan and Sara Sexton Crossan, *Resurrecting Easter: How the West Lost and the East Kept the Original Easter Vision* (New York: Harper One) 45–59.

be shocked at the implications! "The tombs also were opened. And many bodies of those who had fallen asleep were raised up."

After the resurrection stories, more followers dared to see Jesus as "the Lord"—or at least as one with the Lord, which we often translated as "Son of God." This is a clear and dramatic leap forward, an understanding that is fully perceived only after the resurrection, although hints had been dropped throughout Jesus's lifetime. One could say he is gradually being revealed as "Light," which we especially see in the three accounts of the "Transfiguration" (Matthew 17:1–8, Mark 9:2–8, Luke 9:28–36). These are likely transplanted resurrection accounts, as is the story of Jesus walking on the water. Most of us, if we are listening and looking, also have such resurrection moments in the middle of our lives, when "the veil parts" now and then. "Believe in the light so that you also may become children of the light" Jesus says in John's Gospel (12:36), letting us know that we participate in the same mystery, and he is here to aid the process.

My personal belief is that Jesus's own human mind knew his full divine identity only after his resurrection. He had to live his life with the same faith that we must live, and also "grow in wisdom, age, and grace" (Luke 2:40), just as we do. Jesus was "not incapable of feeling our weakness with us, but has been put to the test in exactly the same way as we ourselves" (Hebrews 4:15b), and he can then well serve as our practical model and guide, the "pioneer and perfector of our faith" (Hebrew 12:2).

Back in 1967, my systematic theology professor, Fr. Cyrin Maus, OFM, told me that if a video camera had been placed in front of the tomb of Jesus, it wouldn't have filmed a lone man emerging from a grave (which would be resuscitation more than resurrection). More likely, he felt, it would've captured something like beams of light extending in all directions. In the resurrection, the single physical body of Jesus moved beyond all limits of space and time into a new notion of physicality and light—which includes all of us in its embodiment. Christians usually called this the "glorified body," and it is indeed similar to what Hindus and Buddhists sometimes call the "subtle body." Both traditions pictured this by what became the halo or aura, and Christians placed it around all "saints" to show that they already participated in the one shared Light.

This is for me a very helpful meaning for the resurrection of Jesus, which might be better described as Jesus's "universalization," sort of an Einsteinian warping of time and space, if you will. Jesus was always objectively the Universal Christ, but now his significance for humanity and for us was made *ubiquitous, personal, and attractive* for those willing to meet Reality through him. Many do meet Divine Reality without this shortcut, and we must be honest about that. I cannot prove that Jesus is the shortcut, nor does he need me to, except through the abundant lives of those who sincerely "click on the link" and "follow the prompts." Only "by the fruits will you know," says Jesus (Matthew 7:16–20). People who are properly aligned with Love and Light will always see in good ways that are not obvious to the rest of us, and we still call that "enlightenment."

Such folks do not need to "prove" that Jesus is God, or Christ, or even perfect, as we see in the parents of the man born blind (John 9:18–23). They just need to look honestly at the evidence. Even the man born blind himself says, "All I know is that I was blind and now I can see" (John 9:25). People of the Light will quite simply reveal a high level of seeing, both in depth and in breadth, which allows them to include more and more and exclude less and less. That is the only proof they will ever offer us, and the only proof we should ever need.

In the resurrection, Jesus Christ was revealed as the Everyman and Everywoman in their fulfilled state. As the theologian

St. Maximus the Confessor (580–662), put it, "God made all beings to this end, to [enjoy the same union] of humanity and divinity that was united in Christ".* Later, St. Gregory Palamas (1296–1359) made it even more specific: "God revealed the Christ [in Jesus] so that humanity could never be separated from the pattern that he portrayed."† These kinds of jewels are found much more in the writings of the Eastern church and its Fathers. The great Athanasius (298–373) put it this way: *"God [in Christ] became the bearer of flesh [for a time] so that humanity could become the bearer of Spirit forever."*‡ This was the Great Exchange. Jesus was meant to be the guarantee that divinity can indeed reside within humanity, which is always our great doubt and denial. And once that is possible, then most of our problems are already solved. Resurrection of both persons and planets becomes a foregone conclusion! What that exactly means, of course, I cannot possibly know (1 Corinthians 2:9), but I can say:

> *Creation is the first and probably the final Bible,*
> *Incarnation is already Redemption,*
> *Christmas is already Easter, and*
> *Jesus is already Christ.*

Simply put, if death is not possible for the Christ, then it is not possible for anything that "shares in the divine nature" (2 Peter 1:4). God is by definition eternal, and God is Love (1 John 4:16), which is also eternal (1 Corinthians 13:13), and this same Love has been planted in our hearts (Romans 5:5, 8:9) by the Spirit dwelling

---

*   Maximus the Confessor, *Greek Fathers* 90.621.A.

†   Gregory Palamas, *The Triads*. Translation by Nicholas Gendle. Edited and with an introduction by John Meyendorff (New York: Paulist Press, 1983).

‡   Athanasius, *On the Incarnation* 8, trans. Oliver Clement, *The Roots of Christian Mysticism* (New York: New City Press, 1995), 263.

within us. *Such fully Implanted Love cannot help but evolve and prove victorious, and our word for that final victory is "resurrection."* Peter states this rather directly: "By raising Jesus Christ from the dead, we have a sure hope and the promise of an inheritance that can never be spoiled or soiled or fade away. It is being kept for you in the heavens . . . and will be fully revealed at the end of time" (1 Peter 1:4–6).

Then What About Hell?

One of our biggest roadblocks to this healthier understanding of the cross and resurrection is the prevailing notion of God the Father as Punisher in Chief, an angry deity who consigns sinners to eternal torment and torture *instead of as the one who is life itself.* This idea originates in some misinterpreted Scriptures, largely in the Gospel by Matthew, who likes to end with threats, and also from a phrase in the Apostles' Creed that says Jesus "descended into hell"—so surely there must be one. (He went there to liberate it and *undo* it, like he did the temple, but few people read it that way.) Many of us were taught a vision of God as Tormentor when we were small, impressionable children, and it got deposited in the lowest part of our brain stems, like all traumatic injuries do. So it is hard to talk about hell calmly or intelligently with most people who have been Christians from childhood.

The language of "descent into hell" emerges from two very obscure passages in the New Testament. In 1 Peter 3, we read that Jesus "went and made a proclamation to the spirits in prison," and Ephesians 4 speaks of him descending "into the lower regions." In both cases, the descriptions bear less resemblance to Dante's punitive "Inferno" than they do the broadly used ancient terms for the "place of the dead," like Hades, Sheol, Gehenna, "prison," "among the shades," or even some notion of Limbo.

But Dante's version became the dominant one, forming our Western mind more than any other—even those described in the Bible itself.* Depictions of hell became staples in church art, embellishing the entrances of most Gothic cathedrals, and even providing the full backdrop of the Sistine Chapel. When the message of a punishing God is so visible, dualistic, and frightening, how do you ever undo it, no matter how consoling your sermons and liturgies might be? Even worse, the many Evangelical songs about the wrath of God, along with "fire and brimstone" sermons, often did nothing but reinforce fear of God over trust in or love of God.

If you are frightened into God, it is never the true God that you meet. If you are loved into God, you meet a God worthy of both Jesus and Christ. How you get there is where you arrive.

In the Anglican as well as Eastern Orthodox traditions, the descent narrative takes a slightly different form. It's often referred to as the "Harrowing of Hell," an old English term that meant "to *despoil*" or "to *undo*" something, as farmers in those days did when they flattened out their land with a tool called a harrow. This vision of Christ's descent was summed up powerfully in the Vespers antiphon of Holy Saturday in the Orthodox liturgy, where it says, "Hell reigns, but not forever." Eastern iconography—in contrast with the Western images, which emphasize flames and torture—often pictures Jesus pulling souls out of hell, not thrusting them into it. (Google it if you doubt me.) What a completely different message! No wonder Easter is a so much bigger and more celebrated feast in the Eastern church, where the congregation voluntarily cheers and shouts with delight, *"Christ is risen! Christ is risen indeed!"* (The underlying message is that we are too!)

---

* Jon Sweeney, *Inventing Hell* (New York: Jericho Books, 2014).

In his commentary on the Apostles' Creed, Pope Benedict admits that the phrase "descended into hell" was problematic, confusing, and based on mythological language.* He concludes that if Christ indeed went there, he could have done nothing but *undo the place*; he would have stopped its functioning, just as he did when he "harrowed" the money changers in the temple.† Hell and Christ cannot coexist, he seems to say. We must see Jesus as triumphing over hell and emptying it out. Many of our Easter hymns and sermons actually say as much, but most of us never really accepted the enormity of this message. "He destroyed death," we sing, often without really seeming to mean it.

Such bad theology has its roots in organizing a worldview around the retributive notion of justice, as we discussed earlier, distinguishing it from *restorative justice* (a fancy term for healing). Jesus neither practiced nor taught retribution, but that is what imperial theology prefers—clear winners and clear losers. Top-down worldviews can't resist the tidy dualisms of an in-and-out, us-and-them worldview. But Jesus roundly rejects such notions in both his parables and his teachings—for example, when he says, "Whoever is not against us is for us" (Mark 9:40), and that "God causes his sun to rise on bad as well as good, and causes it to rain on honest and dishonest men alike" (Matthew 5:45), and when he makes outsiders and outliers the heroes of most of his stories.

Desert Fathers and Mothers of the first centuries of Christianity offered a common response when confronted with the notion of a God who eternally punishes his enemies, or the possibility that any of us could experience happiness in heaven while others we

---

* Benedict XVI, *The Faith* (Huntington, IN: Our Sunday Visitor, 2013), chapter 10.

† Hilarion Alfeyev, *Christ the Conqueror of Hell* (New York: St. Vladimir's Seminary Press, 2009).

knew and loved were being tortured nonstop in hell. Some of them said, without indulging in any theological gymnastics, *"Love could not bear that."*

On the whole, we have been slow to notice how God grows more and more *nonviolent* through the Scriptures—or even how this evolution becomes completely obvious in Jesus. Infinite love, mercy, and forgiveness are hard for the human mind to even imagine, so most people seem to need a notion of hell to maintain their logic of retribution, just punishment, and a just world, as they understand it. God does not need hell, but we sure seem to. As both Jon Sweeney and Julie Ferwerda* demonstrate rather convincingly in their respective books, our common image of hell has much more to do with mythological thinking, athletic contests, and punitive practice than with anything representing God's radicality and infinity.

Years ago, when I was a young priest speaking at a Catholic men's prayer breakfast in Cincinnati, I said, "What if the Gospel is actually offering us a win-win scenario?" A well-dressed businessman came up to me at the break, and said in a very patronizing tone while drumming his fingers on the podium, *"Father, Father! Win-win? That would not even be interesting!"* Perhaps he was just being consistent, as one whose entire worldview had been formed by sports, business deals, and American politics, instead of the Gospel. But over the years, I have come to see that he is the norm. The systems of this world are inherently argumentative, competitive, dualistic, based on a scarcity model of God, mercy, and grace. They confuse retribution—what is often little more than crass vengeance—with the biblically evolved notions of healing, forgiveness, and divine mercy.

---

* Sweeney, *Inventing Hell,* and Julie Ferwerda, *Raising Hell: Christianity's Most Controversial Doctrine Put Under Fire* (Lander, WY: Vagabond Group, 2011).

The church was meant to be an alternative society in the grip of an altogether different story line. Restorative justice is used in New Zealand as the primary juvenile justice model, and the Catholic bishops of New Zealand have put out very good statements on it. We see this alternative model of justice acted out in scripture—famously in Jesus's story of the Return of the Prodigal (Luke 15:11ff.), but almost always in the prophets (if we can first endure their tirades). *God's justice makes things right at their very core, and divine love does not achieve its ends by mere punishment or retribution.*

Consider Habbakuk, whose short book develops with vivid messages of judgment only to pivot at the very end to his "Great Nevertheless!" For three chapters, Habbakuk reams out the Jewish people, then at the close has God say in effect, *"But I will love you even more until you come back to me!"* We see the same in Ezekiel's story of the dry bones (Chapter 16) and in Jeremiah's key notion of the "new covenant" (Chapter 31:31ff.). God always outdoes the Israelites' sin by loving them even more! This is God's restorative justice.

Yet we remember collectively the admittedly harsh judgments that usually come earlier in all these texts, which I have to believe was the prophets' own way of teaching the principle of *karma.* (Goodness is its own reward, and evil will always be its own punishment.) This was their way of communicating divine fairness built into our good and bad actions. But the nature of our neurons seems to be that we remember the negative and forget the positive. *Threats of hell are unfortunately more memorable to people than promises of heaven.**

As long as you operate inside any scarcity model, there will

---

* New Zealand Bishops Conference, "Creating New Hearts" (August 30, 1995).

never be enough God or grace to go around. Jesus came to undo our notions of scarcity and tip us over into a worldview of absolute abundance—or what he would call the "Kingdom of God." The Gospel reveals a divine world of infinity, a worldview of enough and more than enough. Our word for this undeserved abundance is "grace": "Give and there will be gifts for you: full measure, pressed down, shaken together, and running over, and poured into your lap" (Luke 6:38). It is a major mental and heart conversion to move from a scarcity model to an abundance model.

No Gospel will ever be worthy of being called "Good News" unless it is indeed a win-win worldview, and "good news for *all* the people" (Luke 2:10)—without exception. The right to decide who is in, and who is out, is not one that our little minds and hearts can even imagine. Jesus's major theme of the Reign of God is saying, "Only God can do such infinite imagining, so trust the Divine Mind."

We Shall All Be Changed

When you study or pray before the Eastern Orthodox icons of the resurrection, you see something quite different from Western depictions. Eastern icons picture the Risen Christ standing astride the darkness and the tombs, pulling souls *out* of hell. Chains and locks fly in all directions across the frame. This is good news worthy of the name. I first felt this leap in my heart when a young Austrian priest came up to me after I had led a male initiation rite near Salzburg. He handed me such an icon as a gift, and said with great enthusiasm, "This is what you are teaching, whether you fully realize it or not." The joy and peace I saw on both the priest's face and the images on the icon showed me what is surely the true message of the Resurrection. As I have said before, but it bears repeating,

John Dominic Crossan demonstrates convincingly through art that *"the West lost and the East kept the original Easter vision."** If that is true, it is a real game changer. In my opinion, we tried to breathe the full air of the Gospel with only the Western church lung, and it left us with a very incomplete and not really victorious message.

"I am telling you something that has been a secret," Paul writes in 1 Corinthians (15:51). *"We are not all going to die, but we shall all be changed."* And he even says "all" twice, but our perversity just does not allow us to see that. Most Western Christian paintings of the resurrection show a man stepping out of a tomb with a white banner in his hand, but in my many trips to churches and art museums around the world, I have yet to see any written words on that banner. I always wonder, Why the empty space? Perhaps it is because we ourselves were still unsure about the message of resurrection. We had imagined that resurrection was just about Jesus, and then found ourselves unable to prove it, nor could we always find this abundant life within ourselves.

But now you have been told about the Eternal Christ, who never dies—and who never dies *in you*! Resurrection is about the whole of creation, it is about history, it is about every human who has ever been conceived, sinned, suffered, and died, every animal that has lived and died a tortured death, every element that has changed from solid, to liquid, to ether, over great expanses of time. It is about you and it is about me. It is about everything. The "Christ journey" is indeed another name for every thing.

As if to confirm this message for me, while writing this chapter on a lovely fall day in New Mexico, I heard the trumpeting and "shouting" of sandhill cranes immediately above my little house. I

---

* John Dominic Crossan and Sara Sexton Crossan, *Resurrecting Easter: How the West Lost and the East Kept the Original Easter Vision* (New York: Harper One) 45–59.

went outside to witness a gyre of maybe fifty elegant birds circling in the thermals of the clear blue sky above me. It was almost like they had stopped on their journey south along the Rio Grande just to rejoice for a while—circling again and again, shouting encouragement to one another and to me. What jubilant noise! After a full twenty minutes of pure celebration, they reassembled into the V formations of their journey, determined to move on and yet clearly in no rush at all, each "announcing your place in the family of things," as Mary Oliver so beautifully puts it in her poem, "Wild Geese."*

I hope many others saw what I saw, enjoyed what I have enjoyed so often, and received what I received. Resurrection is contagious, and free for the taking. It is everywhere visible and available for those who have learned how to see, how to rejoice, and how to neither hoard nor limit God's ubiquitous gift.

---

*   Mary Oliver, "Wild Geese," in *Owls and Other Fantasies* (Boston, Massachussetts: Beacon Press, 2003), 1.

15

Two Witnesses to Jesus and Christ

Among the examples we find in the Bible of who can take us into deeper knowing of both Jesus and Christ, two witnesses stand out: Mary Magdalene, who fully knew Jesus in his humanity and was also the first to see him as the Risen Christ; and Paul, who never knew Jesus in his humanity and almost entirely speaks of Christ. He then becomes the most eloquent witness of this version of Jesus through his many letters. This is the same experience available to all of us, the always-present Christ more than the time-bound Jesus, so Paul is a perfect writer for the New Testament and for all later history.

Magdalene loved a very concrete Jesus who led her to a ubiquitous and Risen Christ. Paul started with a Universal Christ and grounded it all in a quite homely and lovable Jesus, who was rejected, crucified, and resurrected. Working together, Magdalene and Paul guide and direct the Christian experience in truly helpful ways toward both Jesus and Christ, but from opposite sides.

Mary Magdalene

In the Gospel of Luke (8:2), Mary Magdalene is described as a woman who became a follower and friend of Jesus after he had cast seven demons out of her. Not a terribly auspicious start for a person who's then mentioned as many as twelve times throughout the Gospels (more than most apostles). By the way, prostitution is never mentioned as one of her demons in any account. I suspect sex is *our* demon and we projected it onto her.

In all four of the Gospel accounts, Mary Magdalene is said to have been present with Jesus's mother and various other women at the crucifixion (Matthew 27:56, Mark 15:40, Luke 24:10, John 19:25ff.). After Jesus was taken down from the cross, his mother, Mary, and other women accompanied the body to the tomb. (The accounts of which exact women were there are not consistent, but the interesting thing is that it was always women who accompanied the body, with the exception of John's Gospel.) When the Sabbath was over, Mary Magdalene went back to the tomb at dawn and found it open and empty. She hastened to tell two of the apostles this startling news, and they ran to the tomb to confirm it. Suspecting that a thief had stolen the body, the apostles returned to their homes. But Mary Magdalene stayed, weeping and grieving the loss of her beloved friend and teacher (Matthew 27:61). She is the consistent and faithful witness.

In John's account, two angels appear and ask her, "Woman, why are you weeping?" She replies, "They have taken away my Lord, and I do not know where they have laid him." She then turns around and sees a man whom she doesn't recognize. Mary supposes he is the gardener (John 20:15) and asks him where he has taken Jesus. Then, in one of the most dramatic moments in the Gospels, the man simply pronounces her name, "Mary!"

What happens next? Translations say "she turned," or "she knew," or "turning to face him," she cries out, "Rabbuni!" which means "Master" (John 20:13–16). Instantly, Mary sees the one before her in a different way, you might say *relationally instead of merely physically.* She realizes it is still Jesus, but he has fully become the Christ.

In reply, Jesus the Christ speaks a somewhat shocking line variously translated as "Do not touch me" or "Do not cling to me" (John 20:17a). Why would he suddenly give such a cold response? The answer lies in an understanding of the Eternal Christ.

I don't believe the resurrected Jesus was being aloof or rejecting Mary's friendship, nor was he afraid of intimacy. He was saying that the Christ is untouchable *in singular form* because he is omnipresent *in all forms*—as we soon see as the "gardener" at the tomb (John 20:15), as a wayfarer on the road to Emmaus (Luke 24:13), as a man tending a cooking fire by the side of a lake (John 21:4). In each of these inner and outer journeys, Jesus was in the process of returning to his God and Father, whom Jesus tellingly describes as both "my God" and "my Father" and "your God" and "your Father" (John 20:17b). Jesus now speaks from his omnipresent and inclusive Christ role. (I personally suspect this is the same kind of presence that so many people experience right after the passing of a friend, or shortly thereafter.)

I believe that, by repeating "my" and "your" twice, the text is trying to communicate that the event under way describes one common and shared God experience—his and ours. Yes, they are the same experience! You could even say this is the first premonition of what will become the doctrine of the Body of Christ, the radical unity between Christ and all people (1 Corinthians 12:12ff.). Jesus of Nazareth, an individual man, has become Christ, the Corporate Personality.

We used to know him primarily *by outer observation,* but now we know him primarily *by interior exchange.* (Which is how we all know Christ, and is commonly called "prayer.")

Now we can put the whole of Mary Magdalene's story together. Apparently over much of Jesus's ministry life, she had been a frequent witness to the personal, concrete Jesus of Nazareth. But after the resurrection, she also had the unique experience of being the *first witness* to the Omnipresent Christ. Then, acting on his charge for her to tell his friends what she had seen, Mary passed on the good news to the "apostles" (John 20:18, Matthew 28:8). This singular role makes her indeed the "apostle to the apostles," which is exactly how the early church, commentators throughout history, and even early liturgical texts honor her. The first apostle was a woman. And saying that is not trying to be politically correct. It's true by the early definition of an apostle as a "witness to the resurrection" (Acts 1:22).

Like Mary, we must somehow hear our name pronounced, must hear ourselves being addressed and regarded by Love, before we can recognize this Christ in our midst. And like Mary, we usually need to start with the concrete encounter before we move to the universal experience available to all. Spiritual knowing is an inner encounter and a calm inner knowing that we usually identify with "soul" knowledge. We need this intimate inner knowing because *we can't be left at the visual level or we will always think we can localize, limit, or capture God* as a private possession (see John 20:29), or as something that can or must be "proven" to others.

This is no small point. If God is God, then the Divine Presence must necessarily be everywhere and universally accessible. If you can physically "touch" God, it's easy to think God is just here and not there, mine but not yours.

Obviously, Mary Magdalene's unique and important role was not ordinarily acknowledged in the first centuries of almost entirely patriarchal Christianity. Most still imagined that all of the apostles were male, and therefore priesthood and ministry should be reserved for men (as if gender were a quality of the True Self, the restored Self, or the ontological self in God!). This argument is undone, it seems to me, by Christ appearing *first* to Mary after the resurrection, and by his charge for her to be his first witness. Yes, the men ended up getting sent out into the world, no doubt because only men were taken seriously as safe or legal witnesses or even religious teachers in most cultures at that time.

It is also worth mentioning that the twelve men are consistently portrayed in the Gospel accounts as very slow to respond, and usually filled with doubt and hesitation (Mark 16:11, 13–14) and even resistance, denial, and betrayal, yet that is not brought up as an impediment to their leadership. But Mary seemed to recognize Jesus's new kind of Presence the moment he uttered her name. Those who recognize the Presence are the most prepared to talk about it with authority, it seems to me, and not just those who hold a role or an office. But institutions can only survive structurally, it seems, by defined roles and offices. I do understand that.

Still, it is not insignificant that it took a woman who first loved Jesus personally to build the bridge from Jesus to Christ. Mary came to full spiritual knowing quickly because it was a *knowing through love relationship, and presence itself.* Notice that she knew and trusted Jesus's voice, even when she couldn't recognize him. How different that is from our more common empirical knowing, which limits itself to various kinds of "proof," to its own form of reason, and to occasional moments of specific divine revelation. I believe that if we don't learn how to send people on *inner journeys* or *love journeys,* the whole religious project will continue to fall apart, because we have no living witnesses of a transformed life.

I want you to notice that Mary took her journey not by *grasping* on to the old Jesus, but by letting him introduce her to the even larger Christ. In Mark's Gospel this utterly new mode of presence is stated quite deliberately, as it says, "he showed himself under another form" (Mark 16:12). Other texts have him bilocating, passing through doors, walking on water—all indications of a new kind of presence, which we are here calling the "Christ." (Some of these post-resurrection stories are put in the Gospel as pre-resurrection events, like the Transfiguration scene or Jesus walking on water.) We usually have to let go of Jesus on one level before we can accept and believe in "Jesus the Christ." If your Jesus remains too small, too sentimental (e.g., "Jesus, my personal boyfriend"), or too bound by time and culture, you do not get very far at all. For Jesus to become Christ, he must surpass the bounds of space and time, ethnicity, nationality, class, and gender. Frankly, he must rise above any religion formed in his name that remains tribal, clannish, xenophobic, or exclusionary. Otherwise, he is not the "Savior of the World" (John 4:42) at all. This is much of the problem of credibility that we are facing now all over this same world that he is still trying to save.

Mary Magdalene serves as a witness to personal love and intimacy, which for most people is the best and easiest start on the path toward universal love. Then in the garden at Easter, she experienced a sudden shift of recognition toward the universal Presence or Christ. *He, in fact, is the gardener! He has become every man and every woman!* She was not mistaken at all when she "supposed he was the gardener" (John 20:15).

In our second witness, we will meet one who starts with the Universal Christ, which then leads him to a deep devotion to the crucified and resurrected Jesus. God can use either path as long as we stay on that path for the whole journey.

Paul

Unlike Mary Magdalene, the apostle Paul never knew Jesus in the flesh; he only and forever knew the Risen Christ. Earlier we recounted his experience of being struck down and blinded, and we moved from there to consider how his transcendent experience—captured in his favorite phrase *"en Cristo"*—moved him away from narrow religion and into a universal vision. Here I want to focus on how Paul, in effect, started with Christ and rather quickly made a full identification with Jesus, whose *voice* he heard on the Damascus road (Acts 9:4).

Rather than reading Paul's thought primarily as arguments about sin and salvation, as Christians have long tended to do, I want to read Paul as a witness to both personal and cultural transformation, which he himself went through. Jesus represents the personal and Christ the cultural, historical, and social levels. Paul really teaches both, although the second has been largely *under*emphasized until the last fifty years.

You remember that while traveling the road to Damascus, Paul (then known by his Hebrew name, Saul) heard a voice asking him, "Why do you persecute me?" He responded: "Who are you, Lord?" And the Lord said, "'I am Jesus whom you persecute" (Acts 9:4–5). He was struck blind for three days (which often symbolizes a time of necessary transitioning to a new knowledge), and he had to be led into Damascus by the hand. During these three days Paul lived in what I call *"liminal space,"* betwixt and between worlds; he took no food or water from the "old world" he was accustomed to, and began his transition to a "new world" in Christ. His is a classic description of conversion, and it follows the typical progression *from self-love, to group love, to universal love.* But Paul did it rather quickly, whereas most of us take a lifetime. Very soon Paul's "sight was restored" and the hater was baptized into a rather universal love. He became the foremost teacher and proclaimer of the Gospel (Acts 9:17), even more than the original Twelve, and for the rest of his life, he worked to build a solid bridge between his beloved Judaism and this new "sect" of Judaism, as he clearly first saw it (read Romans 11).

The fact that Paul didn't know Jesus in person makes him the perfect voice to name the Christ experience for all of us who come after him. Did you know that Paul uses the single word "Jesus," without adding "Christ" or "Lord," only five times in all his authentic letters? (And two of those appear in the hymn from Philippians 2:10–11, which presumably he did not write.) In recent centuries, Christians have largely read him as if he was focused on what it takes for individuals to "go to heaven" and avoid hell. But Paul never once talks about our notion of hell! Most people fail to notice that. He would have agreed with Jesus, I think, that humans are punished *by* their sins more than *for* their sins. Goodness is its own reward, and evil is its own punishment—although the thought and language of that period led most people to ascribe final causality to God.

If you look at all Paul's texts on evil or "the problem," you see that sin for Paul was actually a combination of group blindness or corporate illusion, and the powerlessness of the individual to stand against it (Romans 7:14ff.) along with systemic evil (Ephesians 6:12 and Colossians 1:16ff.). Evil is not just individual nastiness. "Our battle is not against human forces, but the Sovereignties and Powers that *originate in the darkness, the spirits of evil in the air*" (Ephesians 6:12). We now see that these systems (corporations, nation-states, institutions) have a life of their own, and are usually unaccountable to reason or even law—as much as we try to make them accountable. The ancients were not naïve about such things.

Paul seems to have believed humans are caught in a double bind, and he was convinced that only corporate goodness could ever stand up to corporate evil—thus his emphasis on community building and "church." This is probably why Paul is often called the "founder of the church," and why he expected and hoped for so much from those first Christian communities. He was the proud parent of "children" and exemplars, whom he wanted to show off to the pagans. This admittedly often makes him look didactic and moralistic, which many do not like. But remember, *the greater light you are, the greater shadow you cast.* And Paul is a huge light.

What Paul calls "sin" and personifies as "Adam" or the "old man" (Romans 5:12ff., 1 Corinthians 15:21ff.), many of us today might call *the "human tragedy."* Whatever term you use, Paul believed Christ named the normal human situation as an entrapment, even a slavery, and, like Jesus, Paul tried to give us a way out of what he saw as ephemeral, passing, oppressive, and finally illusory. His vision was not cosmetic but revolutionary, and we miss that if we make him into a mere moralizer or "church man."

I would insist that the foundation of Jesus's social program is what I will call *non-idolatry, or the withdrawing of your enthrall-ment from all kingdoms except the Kingdom of God.* This is a much better agenda than feeling you have to attack things directly, or defeat other nation-states, the banking system, the military-industrial complex, or even the religious system. Nonattachment (freedom from full or final loyalties to man-made domination systems) is the best way I know of protecting people from religious zealotry or any kind of antagonistic thinking or behavior. *There is nothing to be against, but just keep concentrating on the Big Thing you are for!* (Think Francis of Assisi and Mother Teresa.) Paul's notion of sin comes amazingly close to our present understanding of addiction. And he thus wanted to free us from our enthrallments with what he considered "mere rubbish" (Philippians 3:8), which is not worthy of our loyalty. "If only I can have Christ and be given a place in him!" Can you hear Paul's corporate understanding in phrases like that?

The addict, or sinner, does not actually enjoy the world as much as he or she is enslaved to it, in Paul's understanding. Jesus had come to offer us a true alternative social order here and not just a "way to heaven" later.

Did you ever notice that Jesus himself was not really that upset at the bad behavior that most of us call sin? Instead, he directed his critical attention toward people who did not think they were sinners, who could not see their own shadows or dark sides, or acknowledge their complicity in the world's domination systems. Most of us would rather attack an easy, visible target—preferably sex and body-based issues—and thus feel "pure" or "moral." Like any true spiritual master, Jesus exposed the root causes of evil (almost always some form of idolatry), and did not waste time punishing the mere symptoms, as moralistic people usually do.

In his groundbreaking study, *The Apostle Paul and the Introspective Conscience of the West,* the renowned Harvard scholar and pastor Krister Stendahl (1921–2008) writes that Paul hardly ever speaks of personal guilt, or personal and private salvation—we are just trained to hear him that way! Stendahl goes so far as to say that in the undisputed seven original letters of Paul, he does not speak of personal forgiveness as much as of God's blanket forgiveness of all sin and evil. Sin, salvation, and forgiveness are always corporate, social, and historical concepts for the Jewish prophets and for Paul. When you recognize this, it changes your entire reading of the Gospels.

I do believe Paul was implicitly an evolutionary thinker, which he makes explicit in much of Romans 8. Real power is now available and false power has been exposed in Paul's thinking, and now *it is just a matter of time till false power falls apart.* I have witnessed much of this evolution of consciousness in my own small lifetime— toward nonviolence, inclusivity, mysticism, and ever more selfless love, as well as more correct naming of the shadow side of things.

This is the gradual "second coming of Christ." Our present highly partisan politics, angry culture wars, and circling of the wagons around white privilege are just the final gasps of the old, dying paradigm. Jesus and Paul believed this already two thousand years ago, and we are now seeing the inevitable results at an increased pace. Violence is at the lowest rate in all of history, the statisticians say. (What must it have been like before?)

For Paul, it is all a "game of thrones," and there is only one legitimate throne that keeps the smaller kingdoms in perspective and finally losing. "Jesus is Lord" is likely our first simple creed and acclamation (1 Corinthians 12:3), negating the imperial Roman "Caesar is Lord." That is Paul's great and firm act of faith. *These smaller entities have a life and death of their own, and can never be captured by either killing or "redeeming" one individual. Evil was seen by both Jesus and Paul as corporate bondage and illusion, more than just private perverse behavior.* Of course, both are true in the full picture.

Very important, and an utterly new idea from Paul was that the Gospel was not about following some criteria *outside* of the human person—which he calls "the law," but that the locus of authority had changed to *inside* the human person. This is why he rails against law so strongly and surprisingly in both Romans and Galatians. The real and "new" law is an actual participation with *Someone inside of us*: the "love of God that has been poured into our hearts by the Holy Spirit" (Romans 5:5 and throughout). This Inner Authority, this personal moral compass, will guide us more than any outer pressure or law, he believes, and it is available to everyone. This is revolutionary and admittedly scary. As Paul writes in Romans 2:14–15, even "the pagans . . . can point to the substance of the law that is already written on their hearts . . . they can demonstrate the effect of the Law . . . to which their own conscience bears witness." Paul thus provides the headwaters of our still largely undeveloped theology of natural law and individual conscience. He is directly building on what Jeremiah had foretold as the "new covenant" (31:31–34), which would be "written on our hearts." It makes one wonder if most of us are still in the "old covenant" of law and order and merely external authority. Paul was far ahead of most of history, and already pointed us toward what I call "second half of life spirituality."*

Finally, Paul is trying to create some "audiovisual aids" for this big message, which he calls "churches" (a term used by Jesus only *twice*, in Matthew 16:18 and 18:17). He needs living and visible models of this new kind of life—to show that the Christ people really are different from mass consciousness—people who "can be innocent and genuine . . . and can shine like stars among a deceitful and underhanded brood" (Philippians 2:15). In his thinking, we were supposed to live inside of an alternative society, almost a utopia, and from such fullness go out to "the world." Instead, we created a model whereby people live almost entirely in the world, fully invested in its attitudes toward money, war, power, and gender—and sometimes "go to church." I am not sure this is working! People like the Amish, the Bruderhof, Black churches, and members of some Catholic religious Orders probably have a better chance of actually maintaining an alternative consciousness, but most of the rest of us end up thinking and operating pretty much like our surrounding culture. Surely foreseeing this, Paul intended that his new people "live in the church," as it were—and from that solid base go out to the world. We still have it all backward, living fully in the worldly systems and occasionally going to church.

Many people, however, are now finding this kind of solidarity in think tanks, support groups, prayer groups, study groups, projects building houses for the poor, healing circles, or mission organizations. So perhaps without fully recognizing it, we are often heading in the right direction these days. We are creating many para-church

---

* Rohr, *Falling Upward*.

organizations, and some new studies claim that if we look at the statistics, we will see that Christians are not leaving Christianity as much as they are realigning with groups that live Christian values in the world, instead of just gathering to again hear the readings, recite the creed, and sing songs on Sunday. In that sense, actual Christian behavior might just be growing more than we think.

Remember, it is not the brand name that matters.

It is that God's heart be made available and active on this earth.

The direct result of the preaching of the Gospel is, surprisingly, "secularism," where the message has become the mission itself and not just the constant forming of the team. The important thing is that God's work gets done, and not that our group or any group gets the credit. I do encounter Christians who are living their values almost every day, and more and more are *just doing it* ("orthopraxy"), without all the hype about how right they are ("orthodoxy"). Training instead of teaching, as today's coaches often put it.

Just as the Universal Christ moved forward for billions of years without any name at all, so the Still-Evolving Christ continues to do the same. God is quite obviously very humble and patient, and will get the job done without us as his cheerleaders. If God can use a woman with seven devils and a murderous religious zealot to be his primary witnesses, then we had best ask, What were they witnessing to? It was not just some new ideas, it was a new lifestyle, a life energy, a worldview that really believed in "liberty and justice for all."

16

Transformation and Contemplation

The day of my spiritual awakening
was the day I saw and knew I saw all things in God
and God in all things.

—Mechtild of Magdeburg (1212–1282)

If we've been kept from appreciating a cosmic notion of Christ up to now, it has not been because of bad will, ignorance, or obstinacy. It's because we have tried to understand a largely nondual notion with the dualistic mind that dominates Western rationalism and scientism. That will never work. Most of us were not told that we needed to install "software" different from the either-or, problem-solving, all-or-nothing mind that we use to get us through the day. Only early Christianity, and many mystics along the way, tended to understand that contemplation is actually a different way of processing our experience—a radically different way of seeing—which most of us have to be taught.

Such seers were almost always marginalized, like dear Mechtild quoted in the epigraph, whom you may have never heard of. We canonized many of these people after they died, once they were no longer so much of a threat, but many in their lifetimes had to marginalize themselves in forests, practices of silence, hermitages, and monasteries for their own sanity, I suspect. Garden-variety Christianity was quite content with a God figure to worship, and they called him Jesus, with no strong interest in what he really represented for humanity.

As we've seen in the preceding pages, Christ's much larger, universe-spanning role was described quite clearly in—and always in the first chapters of—John's Gospel, Colossians, Ephesians, Hebrews, and 1 John, and shortly thereafter in the writings of the early Eastern Fathers, as well as many mystics along the way. But our noncontemplative minds did not notice that these writers processed reality differently than we do—in fact, very differently. Eventually, such inherently argumentative Christianity jumped the tracks even further. It set us on a very limited "rational" way of knowing that just didn't provide a wide enough lens to process those scriptures or ancient contemplative teachings. It was like trying to see the universe with a too-small telescope. We kept ourselves so busy trying to process the idea of Jesus as the personal incarnation of God, and a God that an empire (East or West!) could make use of, that we had little time or readiness to universalize that message to all "flesh" (John 1:14), much less all of creation (Romans 8:18–23). And surely there was no room for "sinners" or outsiders of almost any sort—which was of course the exact opposite of Jesus's message and mission. Our small empires and our small minds needed a self-serving God and a domesticated Jesus who could be used for ethnic purposes.

This is where a contemplative way of knowing must come to the rescue and allow us to comprehend a cosmic notion of Christ and a nontribal notion of Jesus. It will also help us know that it was not just ill will that kept us from the Gospel, but actually *a lack of mind-fulness* and capacity for presence (along with our cultural captivity to power, money, and war, of course).

The contemplative mind can see things in their depth and in their wholeness instead of just in parts. The binary mind, so good for rational thinking, finds itself totally out of its league in dealing with things like love, death, suffering, infinity, God, sexuality, or mystery in general. It just keeps limiting reality to two alternatives and thinks it is smart because it chooses one! This is no exaggeration.* The two alternatives are always exclusionary, usually in an angry way: things are either totally right or totally wrong, with me or against me, male or female, Democrat or Republican, Christian or pagan, on and on and on. The binary mind provides quick security and false comfort, but never wisdom. It thinks it is smart because it counters your idea with an opposing idea. There is usually not much room for a "reconciling third." I see this in myself almost every day.

In our time, I have been encouraged to see a rediscovery of the broad and deep contemplative mind, which for the first two thousand years of Christianity had largely been limited to monks and mystics. This rediscovery has been the heart of our purpose at the Center for Action and Contemplation, and the core of my teaching over the past forty years. It is not our metaphysics ("what is real") that is changing, but our epistemology—*how we think we know what is real.* For that, we can thank a combination of insights from psychology, therapy, spiritual direction, history, and Eastern religions, along with the rediscovery of the Western and Christian contemplative tradition, starting with Thomas Merton in the 1960s. Now this new epistemology is exploding all over the world, and in all denominations—helping us to so much better understand our own metaphysics! What an irony and surprise.

---

* This is the import of my earlier book *The Naked Now.*

Frankly, a new humility is emerging in Christianity as we begin to recognize our many major mistakes in the past, especially our tragic treatment of indigenous people in almost all the nations that Christians colonized, along with our silence about and full complicity with slavery, destructive consumerism, apartheid, white privilege, the devastation of the planet, homophobia, classism, and the Holocaust. Our dualistic logic allowed us to justify almost anything the corporate ego desired. Now we are a little less arrogant about our ability to understand—much less to actually live—this "one, true religion" of ours. And our critics are not about to let us forget our past mistakes. The harsh judgments of humanity against the actual performance of Christianity are with us for the rest of history. All people need to do is Google, and they will know what really seems to have happened.

It is never a black-and-white story, although our dualistic minds (on either side!) want to make it so. You can, however, know the dark side and history of Christianity and still happily be a Christian. (I count myself among this group!) But it takes a contemplative or nondual mind, which does not allow you denial but teaches you integration, reconciliation, and forgiveness. You must build your tent somewhere in this world, and there is no pedestal of purity on which to stand apart and above. "Blood cries out from" every plot of land on this earth (Genesis 4:10). It is only our egos that want and demand such superiority. Religion tends to start with "purity codes" of one type or another, but it must not end there.

Add to this knowledge of history a growing knowledge of human development, stages of consciousness, unique cultural starting points, different typologies, like the Myers-Briggs, Spiral Dynamics, and the Enneagram. All of these are giving us a much more honest and helpful understanding of ourselves and one another. When we stop our calculating minds long enough to look critically at *how we know*, it is like putting a wide-angle, color lens into what used to be a small, black-and-white camera. We can begin to understand that the Christ Mystery is not something we need to prove or even *can* prove, but *a broad field that we can recognize for ourselves* when we see in a contemplative way, which often will seem more symbolic and intuitive than merely rational, a more non-dual mystery than anything that offers us mere binary choices as a false shortcut to wisdom.

What many have begun to see is that you need to have a nondualistic, non-angry, and nonargumentative mind to process the *really big issues* with any depth or honesty, and most of us have not been effectively taught how to do that in practice. We were largely taught *what* to believe instead of *how* to believe. We had faith *in* Jesus, often as if he were an idol, more than sharing the expansive faith *of* Jesus, which is always humble and patient (Matthew 11:25), and can be understood only by the humble and patient. That's what I hope to address in the rest of this chapter and the next.

Love and Suffering as Ways of Knowing

I hope you will forgive me for beginning this section with a rather absolute statement. In the practical order of life, *if we have never loved deeply or suffered deeply, we are unable to understand spiritual things at any depth.* Any healthy and "true" religion is teaching you how to deal with suffering and how to deal with love. And if you allow this process with sincerity, you will soon recognize that it is actually love and suffering that are dealing with you. Like nothing else can! *Even God has to use love and suffering to teach you all the lessons that really matter. They are his primary tools for human transformation.*

You probably did not realize it at the time, but whenever you were in that honeymoon stage of a new love, you were temporarily enjoying a kind of unitive, nondual, or contemplative mind. During that graced period you had no time for picking fights or being irritated by nonessentials; you were able to overlook offenses, and even forgive your sisters and brothers and maybe even your parents. Mothers think that their sons with new girlfriends have been reborn! They are actually kind, and pick up their clothes; they even say hello and pardon me. I always loved giving pre-marriage instructions because the engaged couples were usually living in a highly teachable time, and nodded in agreement at everything I said. So little pushback.

Conversely, in the days, weeks, and years after a great grief, loss, or death of someone close to you, you often enter that same unitive mind, but now from another doorway. The magnitude of the tragedy puts everything else in perspective, and a simple smile from a checkout girl seems like a healing balm to your saddened soul. You have no time for or interest in picking fights, even regarding the stuff that used to bother you. It seems to take a minimum of a year to get back to "normal" after the loss of anyone you were deeply bonded to, and many times you never get back to "normal." You are reconfigured forever. Often this is the first birth of compassion, patience, and even love, as the heart is softened and tenderized through sadness, depression, and grief. These are privileged portals into depth and truth.

But how do we retain these precious fruits over the long haul? Love and suffering lead us toward the beginnings of a contemplative mind if we submit to them at all, and many of us do submit to them for a while. Too often, though, most of us soon return to dualistic inner argumentation and our old tired judgments, trying to retake control. Most of us leave this too-naked garden of Adam and Eve and enter instead into the fighting and competing world of Cain and Abel. Then we "settle in the land of Nod [or *wandering*], East of Eden" (Genesis 4:16), before we find ourselves longing and thirsting for what we once tasted in Eden. Perhaps we need to wander for a while to find the path—or before we want it real bad.

If we have some good teachers, we will learn to develop a conscious nondual mind, a choiceful contemplation, some spiritual practices or disciplines that can return us to unitive consciousness on an ongoing and daily basis. Whatever practice it is, it must become "our daily bread." That is the consensus of spiritual masters through the ages. The general words for these many forms of practice ("rewiring") are "meditation," "contemplation," any "prayer of quiet," "centering prayer," "chosen solitude," but it is always some form of inner silence, symbolized by the Jewish Sabbath rest. Every world religion—*at the mature levels*—discovers some forms of practice to free us from our addictive mind, which we take as normal. No fast-food religion, or upward-bound Christianity, ever goes there and thus provides little real nutrition to sustain people through the hard times, infatuations, trials, idolatries, darkness, and obsessions that always eventually show themselves. Some of us call today's form of climbing religion the "prosperity gospel," which is quite common among those who still avoid great love and great suffering. It normally does not know what to do with *darkness,* and so it always projects darkness elsewhere. Can you not think of many examples immediately?

Starting in the 1960s, our increased interaction with Eastern religions in general, and Buddhism in particular, helped us recognize and rediscover our own very ancient Christian contemplative tradition. Through Cistercians like Thomas Merton and later Thomas Keating, Christians realized that we had always had these teachings ourselves, but they had slipped into obscurity, and they played almost no part in our sixteenth-century Reformations, or in the Catholic Counter-Reformation. In fact, quite the contrary. Almost all the thinking on all sides has been highly dualistic and divisive, and thus violent, in the last five hundred years. There were no major nonviolent revolutions till the middle of the twentieth century.

When Western civilization set out on its many paths of winning, accomplishment, and conquest, the contemplative mind seemed uninteresting or even counterproductive to our egoic purposes. The contemplative mind got in the way of our left-brain philosophy of progress, science, and development, which were very good and necessary in their own way—*but not for soul knowledge*. What we lost was almost any notion of paradox, mystery, or the wisdom of unknowing and unsayability—which are the open-ended qualities that make biblical faith so dynamic, creative, and nonviolent. But we insisted on "knowing," and even *certain* knowing! All the time and every step of the way! This is no longer the enlightening path of Abraham, Moses, Mary, or Jesus. It is a rather late and utterly inadequate form of religion, and probably why so very many today (half the Western populations?) say they are now "spiritual but not religious." I cannot fault them for that; yet again, I hear remnants of the old dualistic mind.

So Why This Interest in Buddhism?

I am convinced that in many ways Buddhism and Christianity shadow each other. They reveal each other's blind spots. In general, Western Christians have not done contemplation very well, and Buddhism has not done action very well. Although in recent decades we are seeing the emergence of what is called "Engaged Buddhism," which we have learned from teachers like Thich Nhat Hanh and the Dalai Lama. There is a reason that most art shows Jesus with his eyes open and Buddha with his eyes closed. In the West, we have largely been an extroverted religion, with all the superficial-ity that represents; and the East has largely produced introverted forms of religion, with little social engagement up to now. Taking the risk of overgeneralization, I will say that we did not understand the human mind or heart very well, and they did not understand service or justice work very well. Thus we produced rigid capitalism and they often fell into ideological communism. Both religions tried to breathe with one lung—and that is not good breathing. Or better said, *you can't just inhale and you can't just exhale.*

At its best, Western Christianity is dynamic and outflowing. But the downside is that this entrepreneurial instinct often caused it to either be subsumed by or totally trample on the cultures we entered—instead of transforming them at any deeper levels. We became a formal and efficient religion that felt that its job was to tell people *what to see instead of how to see.* It sort of worked for a while, but it no longer does, in my opinion.

I have lived in Buddhist monasteries in Japan, Switzerland, and the USA. They are definitely more disciplined than most Christian monasteries, and definitely much more serious. The first question out of a Japanese abbot's mouth to me was "What is your practice?" The first question when meeting a Christian abbot would probably be something like "How was your trip?" or "Do you have everything you need for while you are here?" or "Are you hungry?"

Both approaches have their strengths and their limitations. In most ways Buddhism is more a way of knowing and cleaning the lens than a theistic religion concerned with metaphysical "God" questions. In telling you mostly *how* to see, Buddhism both appeals to us and threatens us because it demands much more vulnerability and immediate commitment to a practice—more than just "attending" a service, like many Christians do. Buddhism is more a philosophy, a worldview, a set of practices to free us for truth and love than it is a formal belief system in any notion of God. It provides insights and principles that address the *how* of spiritual practice, with very little concern about *what* or *Who* is behind it all. That is its strength, and I am not sure why that should threaten any "believer."

By contrast, Christians have spent centuries trying to define the *what* and *Who* of religion—and usually gave folks very little *how*, beyond quasi-"magical" transactions (Sacraments, moral behaviors, and handy Bible verses), which of themselves often seem to have little effect on *how* the human person actually lives, changes, or grows. These transactions often tend to keep people on cruise control rather than offer any genuinely new encounter or engagement. I am sorry to have to say that, but it is my almost-fifty-year experience as a priest and teacher in many groups.

Transformation, or salvation, is so much more than a favor that Jesus effects for certain individuals in a heavenly ledger somewhere. *It is a full map for a very real human journey. Not really an absolute necessity, but surely a great gift!* And this map is also a participatory experience with a community of some sort, even with the community of unfolding history. I believe the Christian notion of salvation is not just personal enlightenment, but also social connection and communion—which ironically ends up being divine connection too. This alone is full incarnational Christianity, with both the vertical line and the horizontal line forming our central logo of the cross. Never trust only the vertical line or only the horizontal line. They must cross and intertwine and become one. And that is indeed crucifixion.

Spirituality is about honoring the human journey, loving it, and living it in all its wonder and tragedy. There is nothing really "supernatural" about love and suffering. It is completely natural, taking us through the deep interplay of death and life, surrender and forgiveness, in all their basic and foundational manifestations. *"God comes to you disguised as your life,"* as my friend Paula D'Arcy says so well. Who would have thought? I was told it was about going to church.

Authentic Christianity is not so much a belief system as a life-

and-death system that shows you how to give away your life, how to give away your love, and eventually how to give away your death. Basically, how to *give away*—and in doing so, to connect with the world, with all other creatures, and with God.

My Methodology

Epistemology is a science that tries to ask and answer the question How do we *know what we think we know?* Then Christians need to go further and ask, How do we *know what we think we know for sure?*—so we stop producing sterile fundamentalism, so much arrogant knowing, and dualistic patterns of argument. *To be forced to choose between two presented options is never to see with depth, with subtlety, or with compassion.* In our Living School here in New Mexico we teach a methodology that we call our "tricycle." It moves forward on three wheels: *Experience, Scripture,* and *Tradition,* which must be allowed to regulate and balance one another. Very few Christians were given permission, or training, in riding all three wheels together, much less allowing experience to be the front wheel. We also *try to ride all three wheels in a "rational" way,* knowing that if we give reason its own wheel, it will end up driving the whole car.

Up to now, Catholics and Orthodox have used Tradition in both good and bad ways, Protestants used Scripture in both good and bad ways, and neither of us handled experience very well at all. Experience is the new kid on the block. *It was always there, but we did not have the skills or the honesty to admit that we were all operating out of our own experience.* Now we have the tools of psychology and spiritual direction—and Google—to help us trust and critique the always-operative source of experience: the human person that we are.

Mostly, we must remember that Christianity in its maturity is supremely love-centered, not information- or knowledge-centered, which is called "Gnosticism." The primacy of love allows our knowing to be much humbler and more patient, and helps us to recognize that other traditions—and other people—have much to teach us, and there is also much we can share with them. This stance of honest self-knowledge and deeper interiority, the head (Bible), heart (Experience), and body (Tradition) operating as one, is helping many to be more integrated and truthful about their own actual experience of God.

Other Viewpoints

We are also learning from other cultures that we do not "know" or contemplate only by quiet sitting and disciplined posture, which we might have "overlearned" from our Buddhist and monastic friends. After all, Jesus never talks about posture once! In her book *Joy Unspeakable,* Barbara Holmes shows us how the Black and slave experience led to a very different understanding of the contemplative mind.* She calls it "crisis contemplation." Enlightenment or knowledge of God cannot possibly depend upon people who are willing to sit erect on a mat for extended periods—or 99 percent of humanity would never know God. Barbara teaches how the Black experience of moaning together, singing spirituals that lead to intense inner awareness, participating in de facto liturgies of lamentation, and engaging in nonviolent resistance produced a qualitatively different—but profound—contemplative mind that we saw in peo-

---

* Barbara Holmes, *Joy Unspeakable; Contemplative Practices of the Black Church* (Minneapolis: Fortress Press, 2004).

ple like Fannie Lou Hamer, Harriet Tubman, Martin Luther King Jr., Howard Thurman, and Sojourner Truth.

Then there are the walking meditators, like the Russian Pilgrim, who walked all his life reciting the Jesus Prayer, the American Peace Pilgrim, who walked across the United States from 1953 till her death in 1981, and now their modern successors, like Jonathon Stalls and Andrew Forsthoefel, who teach the deep wisdom of goalless walking or "living life at three miles an hour." My own Jesuit spiritual director when I was a young man told me that Type A personalities like myself would do much better with walking than with sitting meditation. Many others come to the contemplative mind through activities like music, dancing, and running. It is largely a matter of your inner goal and intention, and whatever quiets you in body, mind, and heart. As the old joke put it: *It is forbidden to smoke while you are praying! But it is wonderful and meritorious to pray while you are smoking!*

Contemplation allows us to *see* things in their wholeness, and thus with respect (remember, *re-spect* means to see a second time). *Until Richard recognizes and somehow compensates for his prejudicial way of seeing the moment, all Richard will tend to see is his own emotional life and agenda in every new situation.* This is the essential lesson of Contemplation 101, but it does not feel much like "prayer" to the average person, which is probably why many give up too soon and frankly never truly meet the other—much less the Other. They just keep meeting themselves over and over again. In Contemplation 201, you begin to see there's a correlation between how you do anything and how you do everything else, which makes you take the moment in front of you much more seriously and respectfully. You catch yourself out of the corner of your eye, as it were, and your ego games are exposed and diminished.

Such knowing does not contradict the rational, but it's much more holistic and inclusive. It goes where the rational mind cannot go, but then comes back to honor the rational too. In our Living School, we call this "contemplative epistemology." *Contemplation is really the change that changes everything—especially, first of all, the seer.* If I try to "know" or understand the present state of American politics, for example, I only become disheartened, angry, and start making absolute statements, which helps nobody. If I "take it to prayer," as we used to say, I really do receive the data on a screen much bigger and kinder than my small screen, which is always filled with irritating static and electrical charges.

But Why So Much Talk of Suffering and Dying?

My assumption is that Jesus's totally counterintuitive message of the "cross" had to be sent to earth as a dramatic and divine zinger, because God knew we would do everything we could to deny it, avoid it, soften it, or make it into a theory. (Which is exactly what we did anyway.) Yet this is the Jesus message that cannot, and must not, be allowed to be pushed into the background. We believe in a Jesus kind of Christ—a God who is going to the mat with humanity and not just presenting us with a heavenly, cosmic vision. *If Christ represents the resurrected state, then Jesus represents the crucified/ resurrecting path of getting there. If Christ is the source and goal, then Jesus is the path from that source toward the goal of divine unity with all things.*

It is not insignificant that Christians chose the cross or crucifix as their central symbol. At least unconsciously, we recognized that Jesus talked a lot about "losing your life." Perhaps Ken Wilber's distinction between "climbing religions" and "descending religions" is helpful here. He and I both trust the descending form of religion much more, and I think Jesus did too. Here the primary language is unlearning, letting go, surrendering, serving others, and *not the language of self development—which often lurks behind our popular notions of "salvation."* We must be honest about this. Unless we're careful, we will again make Jesus's descending religion into a new form of climbing religion, as we have done so often before.

"Blessed are the poor in Spirit" are Jesus's first words in the Sermon on the Mount (Matthew 5:3). And although Jesus made this quite clear throughout his life, we still largely turned Christianity into a religion where the operative agenda was some personal moral perfection, our attaining some kind of salvation, "going to heaven," converting others rather than ourselves, and acquiring more health, wealth, and success in this world. In that pursuit, we ended up largely aligning with empires, wars, and colonization of the planet, instead of with Jesus or the powerless. All climbing and little descending, and it has all caught up with us in the twenty-first century.

Buddhists talk a lot about suffering and dying, making it its own kind of "descending" religion—even more directly and straightforwardly than Jesus did. "Life is suffering" is one of the Four Noble Truths. But in the Buddhist frame, suffering is not a requirement for following Jesus, not a way to gain merit for eternity, not the proverbial "carrying of the cross" toward salvation, not "no pain, no gain." Instead, suffering is seen as *the practical and real price for letting go of illusion, false desire, superiority, and separateness.* Suffering is also pointed out as the price we pay for *not* letting go, which might be an even better way to teach about suffering.

Any time you surrender a negative, accusatory, compulsive, or self-serving thought, word, or behavior, the Buddhists describe this as "dying"! Power, self-image, and control do not give up without a fight, and this is first of all true inside of our minds, where the illusions begin. Just watch a two-year-old learning to say no to his parents. The battle starts early, comes back in full force in the teenage and young adult years, and in truth never really stops. On a practical level, many Buddhists understood Jesus's words very well, *"Unless the single grain of wheat falls into the ground, it remains just a single grain. But if it dies, it will bear much fruit"* (John 12:24). In fact, they might have understood this message more concretely and immediately than we Christians did! Such daily and "necessary suffering" is the price of both enlightenment for the self and compassion for others. This is what all spiritual masters mean by "dying before you die," or "practicing dying." I myself do not really trust any spiritual teacher who is not up front and utterly honest about a necessary path of descending.

Both Christianity and Buddhism are saying that *the* pattern of transformation, *the* pattern that connects, *the* life that Reality offers us is not death avoided, but always *death transformed.* In other words, the only trustworthy pattern of spiritual transformation is death *and* resurrection. Christians learn to submit to trials because Jesus told us that we must "carry the cross" with him. Buddhists do it because the Buddha very directly said that "life is suffering," but the real goal is to choose skillful and necessary suffering over what is usually just resented and projected suffering. In that the Buddha was a spiritual genius, and we Christians could learn a lot from him and his mature followers. For Christians, of course, the goal is divine love and not the overcoming of suffering. Yet look how many Buddhists become highly compassionate human beings.

Both groups are saying that death and life are two sides of the same coin, and you cannot have one without the other. Each time you offer the surrender, each time you trust the dying, your faith is led to a deeper level and you discover a Larger Self underneath. You decide not to push yourself to the front of the line, and something much better happens in the back of the line. You let go of your narcissistic anger, and you find that you start feeling much happier. You surrender your need to control your partner, and finally the relationship blossoms. Yet each time it is a choice—and each time it is a kind of dying.

The mystics and great saints were those who had learned to trust and allow this pattern, and often said in effect, "What did I ever lose by dying?" Or try Paul's famous one-liner: "For me to live is Christ and to die is gain" (Philippians 1:21). Now even scientific studies, including those of near-death experiences, reveal the same universal pattern. Things change and grow by dying to their present state, but each time it is a risk. "Will it work this time?" is always our question. So many academic disciplines are coming together, each in its own way, to say that there's a constant movement of loss and renewal at work in this world at every level. It seems to be the pattern of all growth and evolution. To be alive means to surrender to this inevitable flow. It's the same pattern in every atom, in every human relationship, and in every galaxy. Native peoples, Hindu scripture, Buddha, Moses, Muhammad, and Jesus all saw it early in human history and named it as a kind of "necessary dying."

If this pattern is true, it has been true all the time and everywhere. Such seeing did not just start two thousand years ago. All of us travelers, each in our own way, have to eventually learn about letting go of something smaller so something bigger can happen. But that's not a religion—it's highly visible truth. It is the Way Reality Works.

Yes, I am saying:

That *the way things work* and Christ are one and the same.

This is not a religion to be either fervently joined or angrily rejected.

It is a train ride already in motion.

The tracks are visible everywhere.

You can be a willing and happy traveler,

Or not.

17

Beyond Mere Theology: Two Practices

Telling is not training.

—Advice offered by executive coaches

You have kindly allowed me to walk you through this Christ journey, and I thank you for your trust. I do believe it has been an act of humble trust on your part. But you might still be wondering, What difference does this make? Is this just more theory and theology? Another set of ideas to put on the shelf? Another well-disguised religious trip?

These critical questions make an important point: Unless the awareness of the Christ Mystery *rewires* you on the physical, neurological, and cellular levels—unless you can actually see and experience it in a new way—this will remain another theory or ideology. Another book you have read and considered, and then forgotten about as the weeks go on. It took me most of my seventy-five years to begin to see and enjoy my Christian faith at this experiential level of awareness. My hope is that I can save you a few of those years, and help you to start enjoying an actual Christ Consciousness much earlier. And as the epigraph to this chapter says, just telling people things is largely ineffective if there is not actual training in how *to practically rewire our responses.* In this chapter I want to offer you two embodied practices we teach at the Center for Action and Contemplation. First, let me say a bit about practice itself.

Practice is standing in the flow, whereas theory and analysis observe the flow from a position of separation. Practice is looking out from yourself; analysis is looking back at yourself as if you were an object. You may learn something intellectually through analysis, but in doing so, you might actually create a disconnect from your deeper inner experience. Until you know what your own *flow* feels like, you do not even know that there is such a thing. And you must also learn to recognize how *resistance* feels. Does it take the form of blame, anger, fear, avoidance, projection, denial, an urge to pretend? You want to spot the clever ways that you personally push back from daily reality, or they will run your life—and you will never spot them. You will think you are "thinking" or "choosing" when you are actually just operating according to program. To get out of your programming is a big part of what we mean by "consciousness."

Foundationally, we must find a prayer form that actually *invades our unconscious,* or nothing changes at any depth. Usually this will be some form of centering prayer, walking meditation, inner practices of letting go, shadow work, or deliberately undergoing a longer period of silence (as I did while writing the first draft of this book, thirty-five days largely alone and quiet). Whatever you choose, it will feel more like unlearning than learning, more like surrendering than accomplishing. This is probably why so many resist contemplation to begin with. *Because it feels more like the shedding of thoughts in general than attaining new or good ones. It feels more like just letting go than accomplishing anything,* which is counterintuitive for our naturally "capitalistic" minds! This is our age-old resistance to the descending kind of religion.

The human need for physical, embodied practices is not new. Across Christian history, the "Sacraments," as Orthodox and Catholics call them, have always been with us. Before the age of literacy emerged, in the sixteenth century, things like pilgrimage, prayer beads, body prostrations, bows and genuflections, "blessing oneself" with the sign of the cross, statues, sprinkling things with holy water, theatrical plays and liturgies, incense and candles all allowed the soul to know itself through the outer world, which we have in this book dared to call "Christ." These outer images serve as mirrors of the Absolute, which can often bypass the mind. *Anything is a sacrament if it serves as a Shortcut to the Infinite, but it will always be hidden in something that is very finite.*

In 1969 I was sent as a deacon to work at Acoma Pueblo, an ancient Native American community in western New Mexico. When I got there, I was amazed to discover that many Catholic practices had direct Native American counterparts. I saw altars in the middle of the mesas covered with bundles of prayer sticks. I noted how the people of Acoma Pueblo sprinkled corn pollen at funerals just as we did holy water, how what we were newly calling "liturgical dance" was the norm for them on every feast day. I observed how mothers would show their children to silently wave the morning sunshine toward their faces, just as we learn to "bless ourselves" with the sign of the cross, and how anointing people with smoldering sage was almost exactly what we did with incense at our Catholic High Masses. All these practices have one thing in common: they are *acted out, mimed, embodied* expressions of spirit. The soul remembers them at an almost preconscious level because they are lodged in our muscle memory and make a visual impact. The later forms of rational Protestantism had a hard time understanding this.

So let's try a practice leading to embodied knowing. I discovered an especially good one in *The Book of Privy Counseling*, a lesser-known classic written by the author of *The Cloud of Unknowing*. I especially like this practice because it is so simple, and for me so effective, even in the middle of the night when I awake and cannot get back to sleep during what some call the "hour of the wolf," between 3:00 and 6:00 a.m. when the psyche is most undefended. (Others simply call it "insomnia"!) I warn you: this pattern gets worse as you grow older, so you will do yourself a favor to learn the following practice early! I have summarized the author's exact words for our very practical purpose here. This is my paraphrase:

Practice I: Simply That You Are

First, "take God at face value, as God is. Accept God's good graciousness, as you would a plain, simple soft compress when sick. Take hold of God and press God against your unhealthy self, just as you are."

Second, know how your mind and will play their games:

"Stop analyzing yourself or God. You can do without wasting so much of your energy deciding if something is good or bad, grace given or temperament driven, divine or human."

Third, be encouraged:

"Offer up your simple naked being to the joyful being of God, for you two are one in grace, although separate by nature."

And finally: "Don't focus on what you are, but simply that you are! How hopelessly stupid would a person have to be if he or she could not realize that he or she simply is."

Hold the soft warm compress of these loving words against your bodily self, bypass the mind and even the affections of the heart, and forgo any analysis of what you are, or are not.

"Simply that you are!"

I like this practice because it can become a very embodied experience of what we've been talking about in this whole book. Your own body—in its naked being, with no "doing" involved—becomes the place of revelation and inner rest. Christ becomes "despiritualized."

Practice II: All Physical Reality as a Mirror

Having looked at the objects of the universe,
I find there is no one, nor any particle of one,
but has reference to the Soul.

—Walt Whitman

As I have often said, salvation is not a question of *if* but *when*. Once you see with God's eyes, you will see all things and enjoy all things in proper and full perspective. Some put this off till the moment of death or even afterward ("purgatory" was our strange word for this). Salvation, for me, is simply to have the "mind of Christ" (1 Corinthians 2:16), which Paul describes as "making the world, life and death, the present and the future—all your servants—because you belong to Christ and Christ belongs to God" (1 Corinthians 3:23).

Everything finally belongs, and you are a part of it.

This knowing and this enjoying are a good description for salvation.

I want to close this book with an extended Mirror Meditation I once wrote. The goal of this meditation is to rewire you—both in your mind and in your body—to see all things in God, and God in all things. I find that if you practice this kind of seeing regularly, it will soon become an entire way of life, in which the natural and physical world can work as a daily mirror for you, revealing parts of yourself that you might not know otherwise, revealing the deep patterns of things, and most of all, showing that what we say about the Christ is true: the outer world is a sacrament of God.

Read this meditation slowly, in parts or as a whole. If you notice that a particular line is speaking to you at some depth, pause and reflect on it until the feeling passes. Don't mistake this sensation for your own thoughts or mere brain chemistry. Instead, receive it as the flow of Divine Love.

THE DIVINE MIRROR

A mirror receives and reflects back what it sees.
It does not judge, adjust, or write commentary.
We are the ones who do that.
A mirror simply reveals.
And invites responsibility.

A mirror, the sun, and God are all the same.
They are all there, fully shining forth.
Their very nature is light, love, and infinite giving.
You can't offend them or make them stop shining.
You can only choose to stop receiving and enjoying.
As soon as you look, you will see they are there!
And fully radiating.
And always have been.
And their message is constant, good, and life giving.
There are only the lookers and the non-lookers,
Those who receive and those who do not receive.

When we learn to love anyone or anything,
It is because they have somehow, if just for a moment,
Mirrored us truthfully yet compassionately to ourselves.

And we grab on to it! Why wouldn't we?
In this resonance, we literally "come to life."
But have no doubt, it is an allowing from our side.
And such pure, unfiltered Presence,
Is accessed only by presence in return.
Nothing more is needed.
Presence comes to us from Christ's side,
And then presence from our side knows what it needs to know.

If that mirror is withdrawn for any reason,
It causes sadness, emptiness, or even anger.
We are normally disoriented, even heartbroken for a while.
We die in some way. But why?
Because we only know ourselves in another's eyes,
We receive our identity—all of it—good and bad,
From another.
The other both creates us and saves us.
"No man is an island, entire of itself," says the poet John Donne.
This is what we call the pure gift of holiness!
Or, if you prefer, wholeness.
We are always a giving, a resonance, never a possession of our own.

The universe is relational at every level, and even between levels.
Relationship is the core and foundational shape of Reality,
Mirroring our Trinitarian God (Genesis 1:26–27).
Every object serves as a mirror, another kind of presence.
You can find such mirrors in all of nature, in animals,
In your parents, lovers, children, books, pictures, movies,
And even in what some call "God."
Remember, "God" is just a word for Reality—with a Face!
And occasionally Interface (which some call "prayer" or "love").

God is a mirror big enough to receive everything,
And every single part of you,
Just as it is, rejecting nothing, adjusting nothing,
Often,
For the sake of an even deeper love.
We will experience a kind of Universal Forgiveness.
A Divine Sympathy for all of Reality.
Or what some have called the "Divine Pity."
And it will even fall on us.
Whatever is fully received in this Mirror is by that very fact
"redeemed."
And all is received whether we believe it or not.
You do not have to see the sun to know that it is still shining.

If your Divine Mirror cannot fully receive you in this way,
Then it is certainly not God.
Remember that regret profits nobody.
Shame is useless.
Blame is surely a waste of time.
All hatred is a diversionary tactic, a dead end.
God always sees and loves God in you.
It seems like God has no choice.
This is God's eternal and unilateral contract with the soul.
If you cannot allow yourself to be fully mirrored in this way,
You will never fully know who you are, much less enjoy who you are.
Nor will you know the heart of God.

Any loving gaze that we can dare to receive can start the Flow:
Creation itself, animals, humans, all are the divine gaze
If we allow them to be.
"The knowledge that I once had was imperfect,
but then I shall know as fully as I am known" (1 Corinthians 12:12b).

One day, the mirror will reflect in both directions,
And we will see over there what was allowed in here.
This is full-access seeing—and being seen:
Most have named it "heaven"
And it begins now.
Let this Divine Mirror fully receive you.
All of you.

And you never need be lonely again.

Epilogue

You can take my word for it too that Greece, Egypt, ancient India and ancient China, the beauty of the world, the pure and authentic reflections of this beauty in art and science, what I have seen of the inner recesses of the human hearts where religious belief is unknown, all these things have done as much as the visibly Christian ones to deliver me into Christ's hands as his captive.

—*Simone Weil*

Afterword: Love After Love

Our unveiled gaze receives and reflects the brightness
of God until we are gradually turned into the image
that we reflect.

—2 Corinthians 3:18

I first encountered Derek Walcott's poem "Love After Love" on the very day the West Indian poet died: March 17, 2017, just as I was beginning to write this book. Back in the early 1970s, Walcott's birthplace, the island of St. Lucia, was the first place outside the continental United States where I was invited to preach the Gospel. In fact, I met him at my conference there, which he was humbly attending! We at the New Jerusalem Community in Cincinnati soon sent four of our young members to work among the poor in St. Lucia, two black and two white, two women and two men. It changed their lives. The beautiful island and people always seemed enchanted to me, and they are still enchanting in my memory. Now you will know another reason why:

LOVE AFTER LOVE

The time will come
when, with elation,
you will greet yourself arriving
at your own door, in your own mirror,
and each will smile at the other's welcome,

and say, sit here. Eat.
You will love again the stranger who was your self.
Give wine. Give bread. Give back your heart
to itself, to the stranger who has loved you

all your life, whom you ignored
for another, who knows you by heart.
Take down the love letters from the bookshelf,

the photographs, the desperate notes,
peel your own image from the mirror.
Sit. Feast on your life.

I hope this book has helped you to experience—and to *know*—that the Christ, you, and every "stranger" are all the same gazing.

Mapping the Soul's Journey to God

In the two appendixes that follow, I present schemas that may help those who still wonder about *how* to frame and understand the Universal Christ described in this book.

Appendix I examines the importance of worldviews, presenting four foundational ones in very simplified form, and an explanation of why I am opting for the fourth.

Appendix II describes a universal process of spiritual transformation, including both deconstruction and reconstruction. Even inside an incarnational worldview, we grow by passing beyond some perfect order, through a usually painful and seemingly unnecessary disorder, to an enlightened reorder or "resurrection."

The Four Worldviews

Each one of us operates out of an implicit worldview, a set of assumptions that are usually not conscious, and therefore are difficult to observe, much less evaluate. Your worldview is not what you look at. It is what you *look out from or look through*. It is thus taken for granted, largely unconscious, and in great part it determines what you see—and what you don't see at all. If your implicit worldview is that there is only the external, material universe, you will quite naturally see things that way without any ability to critique it. If your worldview is exclusively that of a Methodist Christian, you will overlay that Methodism on everything without realizing it—which might benefit your full experience but also might limit it. The important thing is that you know what your preferences and biases are, because there is no such thing as an unbiased worldview. When you acknowledge your filters, you can compensate for them.

I have concluded that there are four basic worldviews, though they might be expressed in many ways and are not necessarily completely separate. Some people represent the best of all of them, or combine several somehow, allowing them to cross religious, intellectual, and ethnic boundaries. There are good things about all four of them, and none of them is completely wrong or completely right, but one of them is by far the most helpful.

Those who hold the *material worldview* believe that the outer, visible universe is the ultimate and "real" world. People of this worldview have given us science, engineering, medicine, and much of what we now call "civilization." The material worldview has obviously produced much good, but in the last couple of centuries it has come to so dominate most developed countries that it is often presumed to be the only possible and fully adequate worldview. A material worldview tends to create highly consumer-oriented and competitive cultures, which are often preoccupied with scarcity, since material goods are always limited.

The *spiritual worldview* characterizes many forms of religion and some idealistic philosophies that recognize the primacy and finality of spirit, consciousness, the invisible world behind all manifestations. It can be seen in Platonic thought; various forms of Gnosticism (which posits that salvation comes through knowledge); some schools of psychology; in the forms of spirituality called "esoteric" or "New Age"; and in the many interior-focused or spiritualized forms of all religions, including much of Christianity. This worldview is partially good too, because it maintains the reality of the spiritual world, which many materialists deny. But taken too far it can become ethereal and disembodied, disregarding ordinary human needs and denying the need for good psychology, anthropology, or societal issues of peace and justice. The spiritual worldview, taken too seriously, has little concern for the earth, the neighbor, or justice, because it considers this world largely as an illusion.

Those holding what I call the *priestly worldview* are generally sophisticated, trained, and experienced people and traditions that feel their job is to help us put matter and Spirit together. They are the holders of the law, the scriptures, and the rituals; they include gurus, ministers, therapists, and sacred communities. People of the priestly worldview help us make good connections that are not always obvious between the material and spiritual worlds. But the downside is that this view assumes that the two worlds are actually separate and need someone to bind them back together (which is the meaning of the word "religion": *re-ligio,* or *re-ligament,* and also the root meaning of the term *"yoga"*). That need to reunite is partially real, of course, but belief in it creates status differences and often more religious codependents and consumers than sincere seekers. It describes what most of us think of as organized religion and much of the self-help world. It often gets involved with buying and selling in the temple, to use a New Testament metaphor. Not surprisingly, the consumers of this worldview fall on a continuum from very healthy to not so healthy, and its "priests" vary from excellent mediators to mere charlatans.

In contrast to these three is the *incarnational worldview,* in which matter and Spirit are understood to have never been separate. Matter and spirit reveal and manifest each other. *This view relies more on awakening than joining, more on seeing than obeying, more on growth in consciousness and love than on clergy, experts, morality, scriptures, or rituals. The code word I am using in this entire book for this worldview is simply "Christ."* Those who fight this worldview the most tend to be adherents of the other three, but for three different reasons.

In Christian history, we see the *incarnational worldview* most strongly in the early Eastern Fathers, Celtic spirituality, many mystics who combined prayer with intense social involvement, Franciscanism in general, many nature mystics, and contemporary eco-spirituality. In general, the *materialistic worldview* is held in the technocratic world and areas its adherents colonize; the *spiritual worldview* is held by the whole spectrum of heady and esoteric people; and the *priestly worldview* is almost all of organized religion.

Each of the four worldviews holds a piece of the cosmic puzzle of reality, and even the incarnational worldview can be understood in glib and naïve ways, and thus also be "wrong." I have seen this among many progressive Catholics, liberal mainline Protestants, and New Agers. When one too quickly and smartly says, "All things are sacred" or "God is everywhere," that doesn't necessarily mean one has really *longed and made space for* this awareness, nor really integrated such an amazing realization. This is why we must balance Christ Consciousness with the embodied Jesus. Incarnation itself cannot become another mental belief system, glibly accepted because it is easy and trendy. Only sincere and longtime seekers experience the deep satisfaction of an incarnational worldview. It does not just fall into your lap. You have to know its deep significance and seek Spirit in and through matter. You really must learn to love matter in all its manifestations over time, I think.

The incarnational worldview grounds Christian holiness in objective and ontological reality instead of just moral behavior. This is its big payoff. Yet, this is the important leap that most have not yet made. Those who have can feel as holy in a hospital bed or a tavern as in a chapel. They can see Christ in the disfigured and broken as much as in the so-called perfect or attractive. They can love and forgive themselves and all imperfect things, because all carry the *Imago Dei* equally, even if not perfectly. Incarnational Christ Consciousness will normally move toward direct social, practical, and immediate implications. It is never an abstraction or a theory. It is not a mere pleasing ideology. If it is truly incarnational Christianity, then it is always "hands-on" religion and not solely esotericism, belief systems, or priestly mediation.

As I have studied the two-thousand-year history of Christianity,

I've noticed how most of our historic fights and divisions were about power or semantics: Who holds the symbols or has the right to present the symbols? Who is using the right words? Who is following the often arbitrary church protocols based on Scriptures? How does one do the rituals properly? and other nonessentials. (This will always happen when you do not know the essentials.) And all of this substituting for—yet surely longing for—in-depth experience of God or the Infinite.

The essential Gospel of *God's loving union with all of creation from the beginning* was seldom believed—and usually actively denied or ignored by most clergy. One wonders, and I do not mean this cynically, if it had a lot to do with job security. We clergy were the needed mediators and salesmen in the other three worldviews, but not so much in the incarnational view. Thus most clergy do not see nature as the "First Bible" but emphasize the much later version, written in the last nanosecond of geological time and then called the *only* word of God. Yet those very Scriptures say that the "Word" was "from the beginning" (John 1:1) and that Word was always identified with "Christ"—which in time "became flesh and lived among us" (1:14). St. Bonaventure believed that *every creature is a word of God,* and this was the first book of "the Bible."*

If my underlying thesis in this book is true and Christ is a word for the Big Story Line of history, then the incarnational worldview held maturely is precisely the Good News!

You do not need to name this universal manifestation "Christ," however, to fully live inside of it and enjoy its immense fruits.

---

* Bonaventure, *Breviloquium* 2, 5.1, 2, ed. Dominic V. Monti, O.F.M. *Collected Works of St. Bonaventure* (St. Bonaventure, NY: The Franciscan Institute, 2005), 72–73.

The Pattern of Spiritual Transformation

Even inside an incarnational worldview, we grow by passing beyond some perfect order, through a usually painful and seemingly unnecessary disorder, to an enlightened reorder or "resurrection." This is the "pattern that connects" and solidifies our relationship with everything around us.

The trajectory of transformation and growth, as I see the great religious and philosophical traditions charting it, uses many metaphors for this pattern. We could point to the classic "Hero's Journey" charted by Joseph Campbell; the Four Seasons or Four Directions of most Native religions; the epic accounts of exodus, exile, and Promised Land of the Jewish people, followed by the cross, death, and resurrection narrative of Christianity. Here, I offer a distillation that might help you see all of these trajectories in a common and very simple—almost too simple—way. Each of these "myths," and each in its own way, is saying that growth happens in this full sequence. To grow toward love, union, salvation, or enlightenment

(I use the words almost interchangeably), we must be moved from *Order* to *Disorder* and then ultimately to *Reorder.*

ORDER: At this first stage, *if we are granted it (and not all are),* we feel innocent and safe. Everything is basically good, it all means something, and we feel a part of what looks normal and deserved. It is our "first naïveté"; it explains everything, and thus feels like it is straight from God, solid, and forever. Those who try to stay in this first satisfying explanation of how things are and should be will tend to refuse and avoid any confusion, conflict, inconsistencies, suffering, or darkness. They do not like disorder in any form. Even many Christians do not like anything that looks like "carrying the cross." (This is the huge price we have paid for just *thanking* Jesus for what he did on the cross, instead of actually *imitating* him.) Disorder or change is always to be avoided, the ego believes, so let's just hunker down and pretend that *my status quo* is entirely good, should be good for everybody, and is always "true" and even the only truth. But permanent residence in this stage tends to create either willingly naïve people or control freaks, and very often a combination of both. I have found it invariably operates from a worldview of scarcity and hardly ever from abundance.

DISORDER: Eventually your ideally ordered universe—your "private salvation project," as Thomas Merton called it—must and will disappoint you, *if you are honest.* As Leonard Cohen puts it, "There is a crack in everything, that's how the light gets in." Your wife dies, your father loses his job, you were rejected on the playground as a child, you find out you are needy and sexual, you fail an exam for a coveted certification, or you finally realize that many people are excluded from your own well-deserved "life, liberty, and the pursuit of happiness." This is the disorder stage, or what we call from the Adam and Eve story the "fall." It is *necessary in some form* if any real growth is to occur; but some of us find this stage so uncomfortable we try to flee back to our first created order—even if it is killing us. Others today seem to have given up and decided that "there is no universal order," or at least no order we will submit to. That's the postmodern stance, which distrusts all grand narratives, ideologies, and globalism, including often any notions of reason, a common human nature, social progress, universal human norms, absolute truth, and objective reality. Much of the chaos that reigns in the American culture and government these days is the direct result of such a "post-truth society." Permanent residence in this stage tends to make people rather negative and cynical, usually angry, and quite opinionated and dogmatic about one form of political correctness or another, as they search for some solid ground. Some accuse religious people of being overly dogmatic, yet this stymied position worships disorder itself as though it were a dogma: "I reject all universal explanations except one—there are no universal explanations!" it seems to be saying. Such universal cynicism and skepticism become their universal explanation, their operative religion, and also their greatest vulnerability.

REORDER: Every religion, each in its own way, is talking about getting you to this reorder stage. Various systems would call it "enlightenment," "exodus," "nirvana," "heaven," "salvation," "springtime," or even "resurrection." It is the life on the other side of death, the victory on the other side of failure, the joy on the other side of the pains of childbirth. It is an insistence on going *through—not under, over, or around*. There is no nonstop flight to reorder. To arrive there, we must endure, learn from, and include the disorder stage, transcending the first naïve order—*but also still including it!* It amounts to the best of the conservative and the best of the liberal positions. They hold on to what was good about the first order but also offer it very needed correctives. People who have reached this stage, like the Jewish prophets, might be called "radical traditionalists." Loving their truth and their group enough to critique it. Critiquing it enough to maintain their own integrity and intelligence. These wise ones have stopped overreacting but also overdefending. They are usually a minority of humans.

Based on years of spiritual direction, with people both in the United States and in other countries, I have observed that the implications of this journey are different for those who identify as either conservative or liberal. Conservatives must let go of their illusion that they can order and control the world through religion, money, war, or politics. This is often their real security system; their intense religious language often shows itself to be a pretense and a cover for a very conservative politics. True release of control to God will show itself as compassion and generosity, and less boundary keeping.

Liberals, however, must surrender their belief in permanent disorder, and their horror of all leadership, eldering, or authority, and find what was good, healthy, and deeply true about a foundational order. This will normally be experienced as a move toward humility and real community. They must stop reacting against all authority and tradition, and recognize these are necessary for continuity in a culture along with basic mental health—which allows them to belong to something besides themselves.

To move toward greater wholeness, both groups, each in a different way, *must let go of their false innocence*. Both liberals and con-servatives are seeking separateness and superiority, just in different ways. In my language, they both must somehow be "wounded" be-fore they give up these foundational illusions. The Recovery move-ment calls this Step 1, the admission of powerlessness.

This journey from order to disorder to reorder must happen for all of us; it is not something just to be admired in Abraham, Moses, Job, or Jesus. Our role is to listen and allow, and at least slightly cooperate with this almost natural progression. *We all come to wis-dom at the major price of both our innocence and our control.* Which means that few go there willingly. Disorder must normally be thrust upon us. Why would anyone choose it? I wouldn't.

I want to repeat that there is no nonstop flight from order to re-order, or from disorder to reorder, unless you dip back into what was good and helpful but also limited about most initial presentations of "order" and even the tragedies of "disorder" or wounding (otherwise you spend too much of your life rebelling, reacting, and suffocat-ing). I'm not sure why God created the world that way, but I have to trust the universal myths and stories. Between beginning and end, the Great Stories inevitably reveal a conflict, a contradiction, a confusion, a fly in the ointment of our self-created paradise. This sets the drama in motion and gives it momentum and humility. Ev-erybody, of course, initially shoots for "happiness," but most books I have ever read seem to be some version of how suffering refined, taught, and formed people.

Maintaining our initial order is not of itself happiness. We must expect and wait for a "second naïveté," which is *given* more than it is created or engineered by us. Happiness is the spiritual outcome and result of full growth and maturity, and this is why I am calling it "reorder." You are taken to happiness—you cannot find your way there by willpower or cleverness. Yet we all try! We seem insistent on not recognizing this universal pattern of growth and change. Trees grow strong by reason of winds and storms. Boats were not meant to live in permanent dry dock or harbor. Baby animals must be educated by their mothers in the hard ways of survival, or they almost always die young. It seems that each of us has to learn on our own, with much kicking and screaming, what is well hidden but also in plain sight.

Bibliography

Alfeyev, Hilarion. *Christ the Conqueror of Hell: The Descent into Hades from an Orthodox Perspective.* New York: St. Vladimir's Seminary Press, 2009.

Alison, James. *Knowing Jesus.* London: SPCK, 2012.

Allies, Mary H., trans. *St. John Damascene on Holy Images.* London: Burns and Oates, 1898.

Athanasius. *On the Incarnation.* Translated by Olivier Clément. *The Roots of Christian Mysticism: Texts from the Patristic Era with Commentary.* New York: New City Press, 2015.

Augustine. *The Retractions.* Translated by Sister M. Inez Bogan, R.S.M. *The Fathers of the Church, Vol. 60.* Washington, DC: Catholic University of America, 1968.

Bailie, Gil. *Violence Unveiled: Humanity at the Crossroads.* New York: Crossroad, 1995.

Balswick, Jack O., Pamela Ebstyne King, and Kevin S. Reimer. *The Reciprocating Self: Human Development in Theological Perspective.* Downers Grove, IL: InterVarsity Press, 2016.

Barfield, Owen. *Saving the Appearances: A Study in Idolatry.* Middletown, CT: Wesleyan University Press, 1988.

Barnhart, Bruno. *The Future of Wisdom: Toward a Rebirth of Sapiential Christianity.* New York: Continuum, 2007.

———. *Second Simplicity: The Inner Shape of Christianity.* Mahwah, NJ: Paulist Press, 1999.

Bass, Diana Butler. *Christianity After Religion: The End of Church and the Birth of a New Spiritual Awakening.* New York: HarperOne, 2012.

Benedict XVI. *The Faith.* Huntington, IN: Our Sunday Visitor, 2013.

Berry, Thomas. *The Christian Future and the Fate of Earth.* Maryknoll, NY: Orbis Books, 2009.

———. *The Dream of the Earth.* San Francisco: Sierra Club Books, 1988.

Berry, Wendell. "The Wild Geese." *Collected Poems, 1957–1982.* Berkeley, CA: North Point, 1984.

Berthold, George C., ed. *Maximus Confessor: Selected Writings.* Mahwah, NJ: Paulist Press, 1985.

Boff, Leonardo. *Jesus Christ Liberator: A Critical Christology for Our Time.* Maryknoll, NY: Orbis Books, 1978.

Bonaventure. *Breviloquium 2, 5.1, 2.* Edited by Dominic V. Monti. *Collected Works of St. Bonaventure.* St. Bonaventure, NY: The Franciscan Institute, 2005.

Bonhoeffer, Dietrich. *Christ the Center.* Translated by Edwin H. Robertson. New York: Harper & Row, 1960.

Bourgeault, Cynthia. *The Holy Trinity and the Law of Three: Discovering the Radical Truth at the Heart of Christianity.* Boston: Shambhala, 2013.

———. *The Meaning of Mary Magdalene: Discovering the Woman at the Heart of Christianity.* Boston: Shambhala, 2010.

———. *The Wisdom Jesus: Transforming Heart and Mind—a New Perspective on Christ and His Message.* Boston: Shambhala, 2008.

Bowen, Elizabeth. *The Heat of the Day.* New York: Anchor, 2002.

Browning, Elizabeth Barrett. *Aurora Leigh.* New York: C.S. Francis, 1857.

Bruteau, Beatrice. *Evolution Toward Divinity: Teilhard de Chardin and the Hindu traditions.* Wheaton, IL: Theosophical Publishing House, 1974.

———. *God's Ecstasy: The Creation of a Self-Creating World.* New York: Crossroad, 1997.

———. *Radical Optimism: Practical Spirituality in an Uncertain World.* New York: Crossroad, 1996.

Buhlmann, Walbert. *The Coming of the Third Church: An Analysis of the Present and Future of the Church.* Maryknoll, NY: Orbis Books, 1977.

Burnfield, David. *Patristic Universalism: An Alternative to the Traditional View of Divine Judgment.* CreateSpace Independent Publishing Platform, 2016.

Cannato, Judy. *Radical Amazement: Contemplative Lessons from Black Holes, Supernovas, and Other Wonders of the Universe.* Ave Maria Press: Sorin, 2006.

Carroll, John E. and Keith Warner, eds. *Ecology and Religion: Scientists Speak.* Quincy, IL: Franciscan Press, 1998.

Chesnut, Robert A. *Meeting Jesus the Christ Again: A Conservative Progressive Faith.* Eugene, OR: Wipf & Stock, 2017.

Chryssavgis, John and Bruce V. Foltz, eds. *Toward an Ecology of Transfiguration: Orthodox Christian Perspectives on Environment, Nature, and Creation.* New York: Fordham University Press, 2013.

Clarke, Jim. *Creating Rituals: A New Way of Healing for Everyday Life.* Mahwah, NJ: Paulist Press, 2011.

Clendenen, Avis. *Experiencing Hildegard: Jungian Perspectives.* Wilmette, IL: Chiron, 2012.

Cousins, Ewert H., ed. *Bonaventure: The Soul's Journey into God, The Tree of Life, The Life of St. Francis.* Mahwah, NJ: Paulist Press, 1978.

———. *Christ of the 21st Century.* New York: Continuum, 1998.

Crossan, John Dominic. *How to Read the Bible and Still Be a Christian: Struggling with Divine Violence from Genesis Through Revelation.* New York: HarperOne, 2015.

Crossan, John Dominic and Sarah Sexton Crossan. *Resurrecting Easter: How the West Lost and the East Kept the Original Easter Vision.* New York: HarperOne, 2018.

Davies, Paul. *God and the New Physics.* New York: Simon & Schuster, 1984.

Dawkins, Richard. "Richard Dawkins on Skavlan December 2015." *Skavlan.* YouTube. December 4, 2015. 14:12. https://www.youtube.com/watch?v=e3oae0AOQew.

Delio, Ilia. *Christ in Evolution*. Maryknoll, NY: Orbis Books, 2008.

———. *The Emergent Christ: Exploring the Meaning of Catholic in an Evolutionary Universe*. Maryknoll, NY: Orbis Books, 2011.

———. *From Teilhard to Omega: Co-Creating an Unfinished Universe*. Maryknoll, NY: Orbis Books, 2014.

———. *The Unbearable Wholeness of Being: God, Evolution, and the Power of Love*. Maryknoll, NY: Orbis Books, 2013.

Deseille, Placide. *Orthodox Spirituality and the Philokalia*. Wichita: Eighth Day Press, 2008.

Dowd, Michael. *Thank God for Evolution: How the Marriage of Science and Religion Will Transform Your Life and Our World*. Tulsa: Council Oak, 2007.

———. "When Religion Fails, Economics Becomes Demonic." *Huffington Post*. May 22, 2015. https://www.huffingtonpost.com/rev-michael -dowd/when-religion-fails-econo_b_7347568.html.

Edinger, Edward F. *The Christian Archetype: A Jungian Commentary on the Life of Christ*. Toronto: Inner City Books, 1987.

Edwards, Denis. *Ecology at the Heart of Faith*. Maryknoll, NY: Orbis Books, 2006.

———. *The God of Evolution: A Trinitarian Theology*. Mahwah, NJ: Paulist Press, 1999.

———. *How God Acts: Creation, Redemption, and Special Divine Action*. Minneapolis: Fortress Press, 2010.

———. *Human Experience of God*. Mahwah, NJ: Paulist Press, 1983.

———. *Jesus and the Cosmos*. Mahwah, NJ: Paulist Press, 1991.

Elgin, Duane. *Awakening Earth: Exploring the Evolution of Human Culture and Consciousness*. New York: William Morrow, 1993.

Enns, Peter. *The Sin of Certainty: Why God Desires Our Trust More than Our "Correct" Beliefs*. New York: HarperOne, 2016.

Everson, William. *The Crooked Lines of God: Poems 1949–1954*. London: Forgotten Books, 2018.

Ferwerda, Julie A. *Raising Hell: Christianity's Most Controversial Doctrine Put Under Fire*. Lander, WY: Vagabond Group, 2011.

Fox, Matthew. *The Coming of the Cosmic Christ*. New York: HarperCollins, 1988.

———. *Original Blessing: A Primer in Creation Spirituality*. Santa Fe, NM: Bear & Company, 1983.

Fox, Matthew, Skylar Wilson, and Jennifer Berit Listug. *Order of the Sacred Earth: An Intergenerational Vision of Love and Action*. New York: Monkfish Book Publishing, 2018.

Francis I. *Laudato Sí*. Encyclical letter, May 24, 2015. http://w2.vatican.va/content/francesco/en/encyclicals/documents/papa-francesco_20150524_enciclica-laudato-si.html.

Galloway, Allan D. *The Cosmic Christ*. New York: Harper & Brothers, 1951.

Gilson, Etienne. *The Spirit of Mediaeval Philosophy*. Notre Dame: University of Notre Dame Press, 2012.

Girard, René. *The Girard Reader*. Edited by James G. Williams. New York: Crossroad Herder, 1996.

Goetz, Joseph, Bernard Rey, Edouard Pousset, André Derville, Aimé Solignac, Robert Javelet, and Albert Ampe. *A Christian Anthropology*. Translated by Mary Innocentia Richards. St. Meinrad, IN: Abbey Press, 1974.

Green, Harold J. *The Eternal We*. Chicago: Loyola University Press, 1986.

Gregory of Nyssa. *The Life of Moses*. Translated by Abraham J. Malherbe and Everett Ferguson. Mahwah, NJ: Paulist Press, 1978.

Gulley, Philip and James Mulholland. *If Grace Is True: Why God Will Save Every Person*. New York: HarperCollins, 2003.

Gutleben, Christine, ed. *Every Living Thing: How Pope Francis, Evangelicals and other Christian Leaders Are Inspiring all of Us to Care for Animals*. Canton, MI: Front Edge, 2015.

Hanson, Rick. *Hardwiring Happiness: The New Brain Science of Contentment, Calm, and Confidence*. New York: Harmony, 2013.

Hardin, Michael, ed. *Reading the Bible with René Girard: Conversations with Steven E. Berry*. Lancaster, PA: JDL Press, 2015.

Haught, John F. *What is God?: How to Think about the Divine*. Mahwah, NJ: Paulist Press, 1986.

Hayes, Zachary. "Christ, Word of God and Exemplar of Humanity," *The Cord* 46, no. 1 (1996): 3–17.

Hillesum, Etty. *Etty: The Letters and Diaries of Etty Hillesum, 1941–1943*. Edited by Klaas A. D. Smelik. Translated by Arnold J. Pomerans. Grand Rapids: Eerdmans, 2002.

Holmes, Barbara A. *Joy Unspeakable: Contemplative Practices of the Black Church*. Minneapolis: Fortress Press, 2004.

———. *Race and the Cosmos: An Invitation to View the World Differently*. Harrisburg, PA: Trinity Press International, 2002.

Ingham, Mary Beth. *Scotus for Dunces: An Introduction to the Subtle Doctor*. St. Bonaventure, NY: The Franciscan Institute, 2003.

Johnson, Elizabeth A. *Creation and the Cross: The Mercy of God for a Planet in Peril*. Maryknoll, NY: Orbis Books, 2018.

Johnston, William. *The Mysticism of The Cloud of Unknowing*. New York: Desclee, 1967.

Julian of Norwich. *Showings*. Translated by Edmund Walsh and James Walsh. Mahwah, NJ: Paulist Press, 1978.

Jung, C. G. *Letters of C. G. Jung: Volume 2, 1951–1961*. Edited by Gerhard Adler with Aniela Jaffé. Translated by R. F. C. Hull. Princeton, NJ: Princeton University Press, 1976.

———. *Psychology and Religion: West and East (The Collected Works of C. G. Jung, Volume 11)*. Edited and Translated by Gerhard Adler and R. F. C. Hull. London: Routledge, 1969.

Kazantzakis, Nikos. *Report to Greco*. Translated by P. A. Bien. New York: Simon & Schuster, 1965.

King, Ursula. *Christ in All Things: Exploring Spirituality with Teilhard de Chardin*. Maryknoll, NY: Orbis Books, 1997.

Küng, Hans. *The Beginning of All Things: Science and Religion*. Translated by John Bowden. Grand Rapids: Eerdmans, 2007.

LaChance, Albert J. and John E. Carroll, eds. *Embracing Earth: Catholic Approaches to Ecology*. Maryknoll, NY: Orbis Books, 1994.

Lanza, Robert, and Bob Berman. *Biocentrism: How Life and Consciousness are the Keys to Understanding the True Nature of the Universe*. Dallas: BenBella Books, 2009.

Lash, Nicholas. *Believing Three Ways in One God: A Reading of the Apostles' Creed*. London: SCM, 1992.

Laszlo, Ervin and Allan Combs. *Thomas Berry, Dreamer of the Earth: The Spiritual Ecology of the Father of Environmentalism*. Rochester, VT: Inner Traditions, 2011.

Leclerc, Eloi. *The Wisdom of the Poor One of Assisi*. Translated by Marie-Louise Johnson. Pasadena, CA: Hope Publishing House, 2009.

Lonergan, Anne and Caroline Richard. *Thomas Berry and the New Cosmology*. Mystic Court, CT: Twenty-Third Publications, 1987.

Loy, David. *Nonduality: A Study in Comparative Philosophy*. Amherst, NY: Humanity Books, 1988.

Lubac, Henri de. *A Brief Catechesis on Nature & Grace*. San Francisco: Ignatius Press, 1984.

————. *Catholicism: Christ and the Common Destiny of Man*. San Francisco: Ignatius Press, 1988.

MacNutt, Francis. *Healing*. Notre Dame: Ave Maria Press, 1974.

Maximus the Confessor. *On the Cosmic Mystery of Jesus Christ*. Translated by Paul M. Blowers and Robert Louis Wilken. New York: St. Vladimir's Seminary Press, 2003.

McFague, Sallie. *The Body of God: An Ecological Theology*. Minneapolis: Augsburg Fortress Press, 1993.

McGilchrist, Iain. *The Master and His Emissary: The Divided Brain and the Making of the Western World*. New Haven: Yale University Press, 2010.

McLuhan, T. C. *The Way of the Earth*. New York: Touchstone, 1994.

Meilach, Michael D., ed. *There Shall Be One Christ*. Saint Bonaventure, NY: The Franciscan Institute, 1968.

Merton, Thomas. *Conjectures of a Guilty Bystander*. New York: Doubleday, 1966.

————. *New Seeds of Contemplation*. New York: New Directions, 1972.

Meyendorff, John. *Christ in Eastern Christian Thought*. New York: St. Vladimir's Seminary Press, 1975.

————. *St. Gregory Palamas and Orthodox Spirituality*. New York: St. Vladimir's Seminary Press, 1974.

Miller, William R. and Janet C' de Baca. *Quantum Change: When Epiphanies and Sudden Insights Transform Ordinary Lives*. New York: Guilford, 2001.

Moltmann, Jürgen. *The Crucified God: The Cross of Christ as the Foundation and Criticism of Christian Theology*. Minneapolis: Fortress Press, 1974.

————. *The Way of Jesus Christ: Christology in Messianic Dimensions*. Minneapolis: Fortress Press, 1995.

Mooney, Christopher E. *Teilhard de Chardin and the Mystery of Christ.* New York: Image Books, 1968.

Moore, Sebastian. *The Contagion of Jesus: Doing Theology as If It Mattered.* Maryknoll, NY: Orbis Books, 2008.

———. *The Crucified Jesus Is No Stranger.* New York: Seabury Press, 1977.

Morgan, Michael L. *The Cambridge Introduction to Emmanuel Levinas.* New York: Cambridge University Press, 2011.

New Zealand Catholic Bishops Conference. "Creating New Hearts: Moving from Retributive to Restorative Justice." August 30, 1995. https://www.catholic.org.nz/about-us/bishops-statements/creating-new-hearts/.

Newman, John Henry. *An Essay on the Development of Christian Doctrine.* London: James Toovey, 1845.

Nolan, Albert. *Jesus Before Christianity.* Maryknoll, NY: Orbis Books, 2001.

Nothwehr, Dawn M. *Franciscan Theology of the Environment: An Introductory Reader.* Quincy, IL: Franciscan Press, 2002.

O'Connor, Flannery. *The Habit of Being: Letters of Flannery O'Connor.* Edited by Sally Fitzgerald. New York: Farrar, Straus and Giroux, 1979.

Oliver, Mary. "Wild Geese." *Owls and Other Fantasies: Poems and Essays.* Boston: Beacon Press, 2003.

O'Murchu, Diarmuid. *In the Beginning Was the Spirit: Science, Religion, and Indigenous Spirituality.* Maryknoll, NY: Orbis Books, 2012.

Palmer, Parker J. *A Hidden Wholeness: The Journey Toward an Undivided Life.* San Francisco: John Wiley & Sons, 2004.

Panikkar, Raimon. *Christophany: The Fullness of Man.* Maryknoll, NY: Orbis Books, 2004.

———. *The Rhythm of Being: The Gifford Lectures.* Maryknoll, NY: Orbis Books, 2010.

Panikkar, Raimundo. *The Unknown Christ of Hinduism.* Maryknoll, NY: Orbis Books, 1981.

Pannenberg, Wolfhart. *Toward a Theology of Nature: Essays on Science and Faith.* Louisville: Westminster John Knox Press, 1993.

Parsons, John Denham. *Our Sun-God: Christianity Before Christ.* San Diego: Book Tree, 2007.

Placher, William C. *Narratives of a Vulnerable God: Christ, Theology, and Scripture.* Louisville: Westminster John Knox Press, 1994.

Polkinghorne, John. *Exploring Reality: The Intertwining of Science and Religion.* New Haven: Yale University Press, 2005.

Rahner, Karl. *Foundations of Christian Faith.* New York: Seabury Press, 1978.

———. *The Trinity.* New York: Crossroad, 1999.

Richard, Lucien. *Christ: The Self-Emptying of God.* Mahwah, NJ: Paulist Press, 1997.

Richo, David. *When Catholic Means Cosmic: Opening to a Big-Hearted Faith.* Mahwah, NJ: Paulist Press, 2015.

Rinpoche, Sogyal. *The Tibetan Book of Living and Dying.* San Francisco: Harper San Francisco, 1993.

Rohr, Richard. *Adam's Return: The Five Promises of Male Initiation.* New York: Crossroad, 2004.

———. *Breathing Under Water: Spirituality and the Twelve Steps.* Cincinnati: St. Anthony Messenger Press, 2011.

———. *Falling Upward: A Spirituality of the Two Halves of Life.* San Francisco: Jossey-Bass, 2011.

———. *Great Themes of Paul: Life as Participation.* Cincinnati: Franciscan Media, 2012. 11 compact discs; 10.5 hours.

———. *Immortal Diamond: The Search for Our True Self.* San Francisco: Jossey-Bass, 2013.

———. *The Naked Now: Learning to See as the Mystics See.* New York: Crossroad, 2009.

———. *Quest for the Grail.* New York: Crossroad, 2000.

Rohr, Richard with Mike Morrell. *The Divine Dance: The Trinity and Your Transformation.* New Kensington, PA: Whitaker House, 2016.

Roszak, Theodore. *The Voice of the Earth: An Exploration of Ecopsychology.* New York: Touchstone, 1993.

Schillebeeckx, Edward. *Christ: The Experience of Jesus as Lord.* New York: Crossroad, 1981.

Seed, John, Joanna Macy, Pat Fleming, and Arne Naess. *Thinking Like a Mountain: Towards the Council of All Beings.* Philadelphia: New Society, 1988.

Sells, Michael A. *Mystical Languages of Unsaying*. Chicago: University of Chicago Press, 1994.

Shore-Goss, Robert E. *God is Green: An Eco-Spirituality of Incarnate Compassion*. Eugene, OR: Cascade Books, 2016.

Shuman, Joel James and L. Roger Owens, eds. *Wendell Berry and Religion: Heaven's Earthly Life*. Lexington: University Press of Kentucky, 2009.

Smith, Amos. *Healing the Divide: Recovering Christianity's Mystic Roots*. Eugene, OR: Resource Publications, 2013.

Smith, Paul R. *Integral Christianity: The Spirit's Call to Evolve*. St. Paul, MN: Paragon House, 2011.

———. *Is Your God Big Enough, Close Enough, You Enough? Jesus and the Three Faces of God*. St. Paul, MN: Paragon House, 2017.

Smoley, Richard. *Inner Christianity: A Guide to the Esoteric Tradition*. Boston: Shambhala, 2002.

Starr, Mirabai. *The Interior Castle: Saint Teresa of Avila*. New York: Riverhead, 2003.

Stendahl, Krister. "The Apostle Paul and the Introspective Conscience of the West." *Harvard Theological Review* 56, no. 3 (1963): 199–215.

Stern, Karl. *The Flight from Woman*. New York: Paragon House, 1965.

Stoner, Gabrielle. "The Alternative Orthodoxy of the Christian Contemplative Tradition." Unpublished Manuscript. Last modified April 11, 2018. Microsoft Word file.

Sweeney, Jon M. *Inventing Hell: Dante, the Bible, and Eternal Torment*. New York: Jericho Books, 2014.

———. *When St. Francis Saved the Church: How a Converted Medieval Troubadour Created a Spiritual Vison for the Ages*. Notre Dame: Ave Maria Press, 2014.

Tarnas, Richard. *Cosmos and Psyche: Intimations of a New World View*. New York: Plume, 2007.

Taylor, Barbara Brown. *The Luminous Web: Essays on Science and Religion*. Cambridge, MA: Cowley, 2000.

Teihard de Chardin, Pierre. *The Divine Milieu*. New York: Harper & Row, 1965.

———. *The Heart of Matter*. Glasgow, UK: William Collins Sons, 1978.

————. *Human Energy.* Translated by J. M. Cohen. New York: Harcourt Brace Jovanovich, 1962.

————. *Hymn of the Universe.* New York: Harper & Row, 1961.

Toben, Carolyn W. *Recovering a Sense of the Sacred: Conversations with Thomas Berry.* Whitsett, NC: Timberlake Earth Sanctuary Press, 2012.

Treston, Kevin. *Who Do You Say I Am? The Christ Story in the Cosmic Context.* Eugene, OR: Wipf & Stock, 2016.

Tucker, Mary Evelyn and John Grim. *Thomas Berry: Selected Writings on the Earth Community.* Maryknoll, NY: Orbis Books, 2014.

Van Ness, Daniel W. and Karen Heetderks Strong. *Restoring Justice: An Introduction to Restorative Justice.* New Providence, NJ: Matthew Bender, 2010.

Vann, Gerald. *The Pain of Christ and the Sorrow of God: Lenten Meditations.* New York: Alba House, 1994.

Visser, Frank. *Ken Wilber: Thought As Passion.* Albany, NY: State University of New York Press, 2003.

von Balthasar, Hans Urs. *Dare We Hope: That All Men be Saved?* San Francisco: Ignatius Press, 2014.

————. *The Scandal of the Incarnation: Irenaeus Against the Heresies.* Translated by John Saward. San Francisco: Ignatius Press, 1981.

Walcott, Derek. "Love after Love." *Collected Poems, 1948–1984.* New York: Farrar, Straus & Giroux, 1986.

Watts, Alan. *Behold the Spirit: A Study in the Necessity of Mystical Religion.* New York: Vintage, 1971.

Weil, Simone. *Waiting for God.* New York: Harper Colophon, 1973.

Whitman, Walt. "Starting from Paumanok." *Walt Whitman: The Complete Poems.* London: Penguin, 1986.

Wilber, Ken. *Integral Spirituality: A Startling New Role for Religion in the Modern and Postmodern World.* Boston: Integral Books, 2006.

————. *A Sociable God: Toward A New Understanding of Religion.* Boston: Shambhala, 2005.

Wilson, David Sloan. *Darwin's Cathedral: Evolution, Religion, and the Nature of Society.* Chicago: University of Chicago Press, 2002.

Wink, Walter. *Engaging the Powers: Discernment and Resistance in a World of Domination.* Minneapolis: Fortress Press, 1992.

———. *The Human Being: Jesus and the Enigma of the Son of Man.* Minneapolis: Fortress Press, 2002.

———. *Naming the Powers: The Language of Power in the New Testament.* Minneapolis: Fortress Press, 1984.

———. *Unmasking the Powers: The Invisible Forces That Determine Human Existence.* Minneapolis: Fortress Press, 1986.

Wilson-Hartgrove, Jonathan. *Reconstructing the Gospel: Finding Freedom from Slaveholder Religion.* Downers Grove, IL: IVP Books, 2018.

Woodruff, Sue. *Meditations with Mechtild of Magdeburg.* Santa Fe, NM: Bear & Company, 1982.

Wright, Wendy M., ed. *Caryll Houselander: Essential Writings.* Maryknoll, NY: Orbis Books, 2005.

Yoder, John Howard. *The Politics of Jesus.* Grand Rapids: Wm. B. Eerdmans, 1994.